Teach
Yourself
to Dream

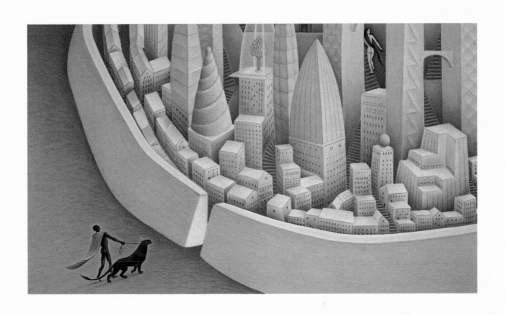

Teach Yourself to Dream

A Practical Guide to Unleashing the Power of the Subconscious Mind

David Fontana, PhD

CHRONICLE BOOKS
SAN FRANCISCO

Teach Yourself to Dream
David Fontana

First published in the United States by Chronicle Books in 1997.

Cover artwork: *Grizelda Holderness*
Cover design: *Rebecca Neimark*

Conceived, created and designed by
Duncan Baird Publishers
Sixth Floor
Castle House
75–76 Wells Street
London W1P 3RE

Editor: *David Gould*
Designer: *Jen Harte*
Commissioned artwork: *Hugh Dixon, Grizelda Holderness*
Picture research: *Jan Croot*

Typeset in Perpetua
Colour reproduction by Colourscan, Singapore
Printed in USA

ISBN 0-8118-1628-1

Distributed in Canada by
Raincoast Books
8680 Cambie Street
Vancouver, B.C. V6P 6M9

Chronicle Books
85 Second Street
San Francisco, CA 94105

*" If we heed the lessons of our dreams, we will no longer
be dominated by the mundane events of the day.
We will regain the wholeness that is our birthright. "*

Contents

Introducing the Dream World

*"A dream is a theatre in which the dreamer himself is the
scene, the player, the prompter, the producer, the author, the
public and the critic."*
Carl Jung

Why should we teach ourselves to dream? Why attach any
importance to the apparently random jumble of memories,
fantasies and absurdities that make up our dreams? The answer
is that, although we dream every night, we often fail to grasp
the unique importance of our nightly experiences. Dreams are
our chance to eavesdrop on a conversation between our unconscious and conscious minds, offering us opportunities to understand ourselves better and achieve greater inner harmony.

In the pages that follow, you will find a wide range of tried
and tested techniques to reach these goals. We can learn how
to reveal the special personal meanings of our dreams, and how
to make them more vivid. We can ask our unconscious to help
us solve practical problems and to show us a way forward in
times of personal difficulty, and we can even teach ourselves
to lucid-dream – to take control of our dreams.

This book sets out to help you to understand the purpose of
dreaming, and to enhance your ability to recall and interpret
dreams. It will show that dreams are an integral part of mental
life, and show how you can work with them to gain vital self-
understanding; and because dreaming is an essentially visual
activity, the illustrations are designed as a further way to prompt richness and colour in
your dream experiences.

Approaching the Dream World

"And dreams in their development have breath,
And tears and torture and a touch of joy."
Lord Byron

All through history, people have been fascinated by dreams, and in many ways men and women of the past were more skilled in their use and interpretation than we are now.

The scientific study of dreams is less than 50 years old. It started with the work of American scientists Nathaniel Kleitman and Eugene Aserinsky, who discovered that volunteers who were woken while their brains were exhibiting specific rhythms reported that they had been dreaming. William Dement, a psychologist working at the University of Chicago, was another key figure in the new science of dream studies. He detected links between the content of dreams and the psychological condition of the dreamer, and convincingly demonstrated how inadequately most people recall their dreams. We can remember about 80 per cent of each dream episode if we are roused immediately after its completion, but this falls to about 30 per cent in the next eight minutes or so, and then rapidly to about five per cent.

Research is now focusing on a wide range of factors associated with dreaming, including the influence of pre-sleep experiences, the creative power of dreams, and even apparent dreaming episodes in babies and animals. The quest to understand our dreams is once again being taken seriously.

Learning from History

Dream Cue
_____

*As a way to induce
dreams of other
times, think about a
time and place you
would like to have
lived in — perhaps
ancient Greece, or
the Wild West.
Before you go to
sleep, ask to be
transported there.*

Dreaming is an intrinsic part of all our lives: it is one of the common strands that unites all human beings, a rich and rewarding example of the gifts that we can encounter if we approach all experiences of the mind without prejudice or scepticism.

In ancient times, it was widely believed that dreams had the power to solve problems, enhance fertility, bring hunters prowess and make warriors bold and skilful. Dreams could also predict the future, heal sickness and bring spiritual revelation. Our forebears constantly sought to "incubate" dreams that would bring such blessings. To this end, they slept in sacred or lonely places (in temples or in the wilderness) and followed distinctive rituals to make requests for dreams. These physical and spiritual disciplines made them mentally prepared and especially receptive to vivid dreams.

The ancient Greeks' knowledge of the potential of dreams, like their knowledge in so many fields, was especially sophisticated. Socrates (*c.*470–399BC) anticipated Freud by more than two thousand years when he explained that dreams were a place where a person's bestial desires run riot, unless the "well-governed soul" is able to replace baser instincts with reason, in which case dreams equip us to come "nearer to grasping the truth than at any other time". Aristotle (384–322BC) said that the insights available from dreams were like objects reflected in water: when the water is calm, the forms are easy to see; when the water is agitated (that is, when the mind is emotionally disturbed), the reflections become distorted and meaningless. The more the mind can be stilled before sleep, said Aristotle, the more the dreamer can learn.

*Ancient
Egyptians would
pray to the god Bes,
protector of families
– portrayed here on
a tile – for
untroubled dreams.*

The practice of sleeping at holy places to bring on particular types of dreams was common in Greece and throughout pagan Europe. Perhaps surprisingly, early Christians followed the same procedure, sleeping at shrines of saints or martyrs who could send dreams with the power to heal or bring peace.

In the Far East, too, there were temples for dreamers. For example, in 14th-century China, each city was watched over by its own god. When visiting a city, government officials had to spend their first night in the temple, waiting for instructions from the god. Judges also slept in the temple to receive guidance, first purifying themselves by fasting and ritual bathing, then burning a written petition before the altar to inform the god of all the relevant legal arguments.

The idea that dreams could supply missing links, helping us to solve problems and make decisions, has not been confined to ancient cultures. Even René Descartes (1596–1650), the French philosopher who is considered one of the founders of modern science, believed in "priming" the mind to incubate meaningful dreams. Descartes said that several of his major theories came to him in dreams, and in his philosophy he struggled to find a clear distinction between dreaming and waking experience, concluding that "even if I were asleep, everything that appears evident to my mind is absolutely true".

Gaining access to the meaning of dreams, and finding the truth that emerges from the deep wells of our unconscious, is one of the main aims of this book. Many of the best techniques for influencing our dreams owe as much to the wisdom of the past as to the discoveries of modern science, and we will explore some of them as we teach ourselves to dream.

The ancient Greeks were firm believers in the power of dreams to change lives. Hypnos, the god of sleep depicted here, was an important figure in the Greek dream world.

Stages of Sleep

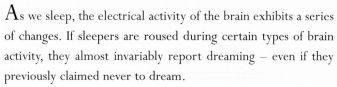

A night's sleep usually passes through at least four episodes of vivid dreaming, indicated here by milestones.

As we sleep, the electrical activity of the brain exhibits a series of changes. If sleepers are roused during certain types of brain activity, they almost invariably report dreaming – even if they previously claimed never to dream.

Much of our memorable dreaming takes place during what is known as Rapid Eye Movement (REM) sleep, a stage marked by 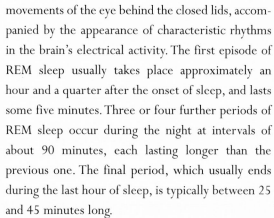 movements of the eye behind the closed lids, accompanied by the appearance of characteristic rhythms in the brain's electrical activity. The first episode of REM sleep usually takes place approximately an hour and a quarter after the onset of sleep, and lasts some five minutes. Three or four further periods of REM sleep occur during the night at intervals of about 90 minutes, each lasting longer than the previous one. The final period, which usually ends during the last hour of sleep, is typically between 25 and 45 minutes long.

REM sleep is important for our psychological health. If we are deprived of it, we suffer from daytime memory loss, poor concentration, fatigue and irritability, and try to make up the deficit by increasing the time spent in REM sleep on subsequent nights. Total sleep deprivation can even lead to episodes of REM brain activity (often complete with accompanying dream images and emotions) while we are still awake. It may not be over-fanciful to propose that one of the reasons we sleep is in order to dream.

Research shows that we normally experience the vivid dreams associated with REM sleep for a total of around two hours each night. Dreams are not, however, confined to this type of sleep. Up to 7 times out of 10, light sleepers roused during non-REM sleep report dreams that seem little different from REM dreams. Heavier sleepers dream less during non-REM sleep, and the dreams they do have are less visual and active than REM dreams, and are in many ways more akin to thinking. For many of us there are few, if any, periods during sleep when our minds are not active. To ignore our dreams, then, may be to ignore a large part of our mental lives.

Dreaming embraces the body as well as the brain. Even during apparently tranquil dreams, the nervous system responds by increasing heart rate, breathing and gastric secretions. We also show signs of sexual arousal even when erotic dream content is absent. At the same time, as if we recognize the dangers that could arise from any attempt to act out dream events physically, we lose muscle tone, resulting in effective paralysis of all major muscle groups except those involved in eye movements. In short, we become totally involved in our dreams.

While scientists generally agree that the *process* of dreaming is important, many of them believe that the *content* is valueless. In their view, dreams are simply the meaningless jumble that passes through the brain as it scrutinizes the mass of material that has bombarded it during the day, dumping unwanted memories much as a computer might delete redundant data at the end of a session. However, the coherence of much dream material and the existence of recurring dreams, which repeat themselves over many years, would suggest otherwise. The appearance in dreams of memories from long ago, and the proven therapeutic value of dream interpretation, confirm that the dreaming mind can give us valuable guidance.

Rapid movement *of the eyes during periods of vivid dreaming suggests that the sleeper may be attempting to follow the events of the dream.*

Why Do We Sleep?

There are many theories as to why we sleep. Some scientists point to the evolutionary advantage of sleep as a strategy to conserve energy and reduce food consumption. Another evolutionary argument is that by sleeping during the hours of darkness, when they were more vulnerable to attack from predators, our ancestors increased their chances of survival. A physiological theory suggests that sleep is the body's chance to relax and repair itself, and to use its energies to secrete special hormones: children, for example, produce more abundant supplies of growth hormone at night.

Even during light sleep, the mind relaxes its grip on the imagination, setting it free to take flight.

It seems certain that sleep literally gives the brain a rest. Production of serotonin and norepinephrine, chemicals that help to transmit nerve impulses in the brain, is reduced during sleep. Volunteers deprived of one or two nights' sleep show increased irritability, memory failure and poor concentration, and will literally pass out on their feet if deprivation continues. Nevertheless, some people need very little sleep, and certain spiritually advanced men and women pass the night in a state of deep meditation rather than actual sleep. There are rare medical cases of people who, after traumas such as head injuries, appear hardly to sleep at all.

Sleep is the arena in which our nightly dreams are played out. As a first step toward teaching ourselves to dream, we can take a few simple measures to teach ourselves to sleep.

Guidelines for Better Sleep

Many unsuccessful dreamers first need help with sleep problems. Most drugs taken for insomnia suppress REM sleep, and therefore dream episodes; alcohol does the same. The best way to tackle insomnia is by natural means, here summarized as 10 simple rules.

1 *Clear your mind of all the anxieties and thoughts of the day. Avoid feelings of anger or resentment, which can be more potent than anxiety in maintaining wakefulness.*

2 *Don't read an exciting book or watch a thrilling film before bedtime. Excitement is another obstacle to sleep.*

3 *Tell yourself frequently during the day, and again last thing at night, that you will relax in mind and body, go to sleep quickly, and sleep right through to the morning.*

4 *Make the bedroom a pleasant place, softly-lit, quiet and comfortable.*

5 *Follow the natural human sleep pattern by retiring early and waking early.*

6 *Unwind physically. Progressively relax your body, tensing and then releasing each group of muscles from the toes to the head. Alternatively, meditate for at least fifteen minutes before retiring.*

7 *Avoid nicotine and caffeine for at least an hour before bedtime — they both harm sleep. In small amounts alcohol, which is a depressant, can help you get to sleep, but it is better not to rely on it.*

8 *Try hot milk and honey or a malted milk drink as a soothing bedtime beverage.*

9 *Repeat a soothing formula — such as "I am drifting off to sleep"— before sleep and if you wake during the night. Alternatively, repeat a peaceful visual exercise, such as visualizing trees waving in the breeze. You could even use the old trick of counting sheep. If these exercises produce no immediate effect, persevere with them. After several nights the unconscious will begin to get the message.*

10 *Don't worry about the amount you are sleeping — in the end, our bodies make sure we get all the sleep we need. Worrying or annoyance because you can't sleep is a guarantee of wakefulness.*

Between Sleep and Waking

Dream Cue

Try taking a nap sitting bolt upright instead of lying down. This can easily be done on trains, planes or as a car passenger. As you nod off, your head will jerk forward and wake you up. This is a good way to skirt the borders of sleep, where hypnagogic visions can be found.

Sleep and wakefulness are not rigidly divided from each other. They are bridged by two transitional half-worlds, elusive, fragmentary and almost as enigmatic as the dream world itself. The hypnagogic state occurs between waking and sleeping, and the hypnopompic state takes place as we emerge from sleep into wakefulness. Both are characterized by a succession of fleeting visions and strange images, often of great beauty.

Many hypnagogic and hypnopompic images bear no relation to waking memories, and are similar to images that appear at various stages of meditation, suggesting that they arise from a deep level of the creative unconscious. They were certainly an important source of inspiration for surrealist artists, such as Salvador Dalí and René Magritte.

Train yourself to experience hypnagogic images by deliberately preventing yourself from falling fully asleep. Keep half your attention on a stimulus such as music or a television program during periods of sleepiness, and allow your mind to drift. Notice how your attention moves between different levels of consciousness, producing vivid thoughts and strange visions which seem suddenly to spring up before your eyes.

When you go to bed, enable a relaxed watchfulness to develop by allowing the centre of your thoughts to rest lightly on an inner space behind the eyelids. Allow images to arise in their own time. The first ones may be faint and fleeting and easily missed, so you should pay close attention. Allow the images to appear and fade as if they have a life of their own.

If, despite your best efforts, you still fall asleep before hypnagogic visions appear, try using a Tibetan technique to elicit them.
Imagine a spinning disk of light behind your eyelids or at the
heart, through which images from your unconscious will flash
through. A Buddhist sage, an animal, a face, a haunting landscape
– each image will be completely personal to you. If you still find
that you are not experiencing hypnagogic images, conjure them
up yourself: ask your dozing mind for the images you would like
to see, or imagine numbers or the letters of the alphabet in
sequence – these can often transform themselves into geometrical images, which in turn spontaneously stimulate typical hypnagogic visions.

Sometimes frightening apparitions dominate the hypnagogic
state. If such alarming images persist, banish them by imagining
in their place a mandala (concentric meditation symbol), or a
special symbol that has pleasant associations for you. If you deliberately push the images away, you will only be acknowledging
their importance; and as a result, you might paradoxically be
strengthening their hold.

*Strange
landscapes of
places you have never
seen can flash before
your eyes as you drift
off to sleep.*

21

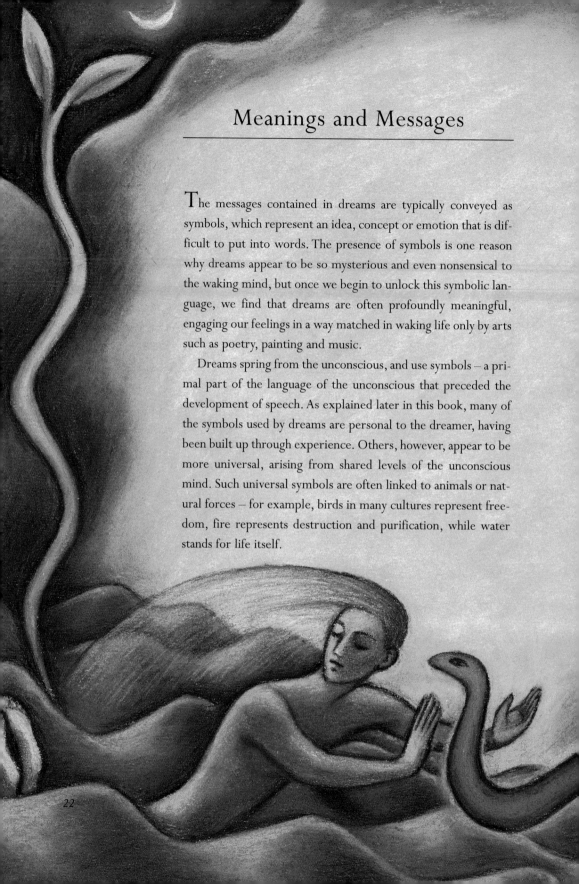

Meanings and Messages

The messages contained in dreams are typically conveyed as symbols, which represent an idea, concept or emotion that is difficult to put into words. The presence of symbols is one reason why dreams appear to be so mysterious and even nonsensical to the waking mind, but once we begin to unlock this symbolic language, we find that dreams are often profoundly meaningful, engaging our feelings in a way matched in waking life only by arts such as poetry, painting and music.

Dreams spring from the unconscious, and use symbols – a primal part of the language of the unconscious that preceded the development of speech. As explained later in this book, many of the symbols used by dreams are personal to the dreamer, having been built up through experience. Others, however, appear to be more universal, arising from shared levels of the unconscious mind. Such universal symbols are often linked to animals or natural forces – for example, birds in many cultures represent freedom, fire represents destruction and purification, while water stands for life itself.

By working with dreams, we come into contact with this symbolic language, which shows us a way to delve deeper and deeper into the unconscious, enabling us to embark on a thrilling (and sometimes disturbing) voyage of self-discovery. We could be given any message on the way, and its special meaning will depend on our particular personal agenda, fears and other inner concerns.

Many of the messages we receive in dreams are connected with the hopes, concerns and anxieties of everyday life. Research has shown that women's dreams tend to focus on domestic events, while men's dreams are more often set outside the home. Many dreams, however, arise from deeper levels of the mind (see page 24). Before attempting the methods of interpretation explained later in this book, ask yourself what message each remembered dream *might* be attempting to convey. For example, you may have had dreams of meeting a stranger, entering a store, or chopping down a tree. What could such dreams be trying to say?

In a broad sense, dreams often relate to what might be, rather than what actually is. A dream could thus suggest that you might wish to enlarge your horizons, or to explore new avenues and opportunities. Sometimes dreams seem to warn us of dangers, or to caution us to think more carefully about a particular course of action. The one clear message is that dreams are far too important to be ignored.

The Dream Experience

Many people experience a rich dream life. Others report dreamless sleep night after night. However, the world is not divided into dreamers and non-dreamers: everyone dreams every night. The difference is that some people have few problems remembering their dreams, while for others, who for some reason are less adept at dream recall, the hours of sleep represent total oblivion. Using the techniques outlined in the next chapter, there is no reason why anyone should fail to recall at least some part of their dream experiences upon waking.

A first step in understanding the nature of these experiences is to recognize that they stem from different levels of the unconscious. Sigmund Freud, who did much to draw scientific attention to dreams, suggested that the unconscious mind consists of two levels: the "preconscious" and the "personal unconscious". To these Carl Jung added a third level, the "collective unconscious". To both Freud and Jung, and to more recent schools of psychotherapy, these levels represent successively deeper strata of the mind, exerting a powerful though usually unrecognized influence upon our conscious behaviour. By offering new insights from each of these levels, and increasing our awareness of them, dreams often provide a vital avenue toward self-understanding.

Any dream can contain material from more than one level, but typically one or other level predominates, guiding the way in which we approach each dream. Dreams from the preconscious, for example, are really a continuation of waking preoccupations, weaving together fragments of recent events, current anxieties and acknowledged hopes and wishes. The meaning of such dreams can often be taken at face value.

Dream Cue

Think of the mind as a tall building. We spend most of the time on the top floor – the domain of the conscious mind. Occasionally, however, we go down onto the lower levels, which represent the unconscious. Hold the image of this building in the mind before sleep, instructing your dreams to roam freely through it in search of meaning.

Levels of Meaning

Dreams come from different levels of the unconscious. These can be described as:

Level 1 – *the preconscious: the most accessible part of our mind, containing all the material that can readily be called into consciousness when we are awake.*

Level 2 – *the personal unconscious: memories that are beyond the reach of our waking consciousness, but exert a profound influence upon our psychological life, including our dream life. Childhood traumas, repressed wishes and fears, unacknowledged emotions and expectations, all form part of our personal unconscious, which develops and changes over time.*

Level 3 – *the collective unconscious: the primal ideas, symbols, themes and archetypes forming the raw material for profound human aspirations, drives and longings. The collective unconscious is an inherited level of mind, common to us all, from which come the recurring themes in the myths and legends of all cultures. Jung referred to the collective unconscious as "the vast historical storehouse of the human race".*

Because Level 1 dreams revolve around the mundane events of the day, they can deceive us into thinking that they are meaningless. However, everything we dream is significant, and we should ask why the dreaming mind has selected trivia instead of deeper concerns. The dream may, in fact, be using trivial events as an indirect means of addressing Level 2 or 3 material that is more difficult to access directly. A dream might, for example, replay the recent unmemorable experience of calling a wrong telephone number as a way to represent a deep and unrecognized fear of failure to communicate one's deeper self to others. In this way, apparently inconsequential Level 1 material can serve to unlock some profound Level 2 messages during dream interpretation.

Level 2 dreams are often concerned with long-lost memories and deep personal issues. They frequently feature situations and events quite foreign to waking life. The dreamer may find himself or herself in a strange role or an unfamiliar situation, relating to unknown people or behaving entirely out of character. The dream may have an intriguing feel about it, and stay in the memory as if asking insistently for interpretation. From the most unlikely starting point, careful analysis and interpretation may eventually uncover the most revealing inner material.

Level 1 dreams seem to be straightforward rehearsals of waking concerns, but they often mask or reveal deeper concerns.

Usually the symbolism of Level 2 dreams is personal to the dreamer, which is one reason why dream dictionaries containing standard meanings for each symbol are of little use. A dream of a clothes store, for example, may symbolize for one person the childhood wish to have new clothes instead of garments handed down from older siblings, and thus reflect unacknowledged feelings of inferiority or resentment. For another it may be linked with an early memory of humiliation at knocking over a clothes stand during a forbidden game of chase while a parent was busy in the fitting room.

Level 3 dreams – generally the rarest – deal with profound themes such as spirituality, life and death, transformation, love, sacrifice and heroism. Typically the symbols operating at this level are universal, and can often best be understood by studying their appearance in the myths and legends of one's own or other people's culture – a technique known as "amplification" (see page 96). Jung referred to such dreams as "grand dreams", and pointed to their appearance at key transitional stages in life, and to their ability to retain their freshness and power in the memory over the years.

Level 2 dreams involve material from the personal unconscious.

Level 3 dreams reflect the deep concerns of the collective unconscious.

Individuals experience wide variations in the number and ratio of dreams from each of the three different levels. People who are engaged in self-exploration practices such as meditation, or are involved in psychotherapy, generally report an increase in

Level 3 dreams. Distinctive rhythms in the nightly dream cycle may generate particular types of dreams at particular times, swaying each dreamer's perception of his or her dream life. You can explore these rhythms by setting an alarm clock to awaken yourself at various points during the night, and by recording the dream memories each time you wake up. You might find, for example, that your most vivid and meaningful dreams occur in the early hours of the morning and are normally lost to the memory.

Warnings and Precognition

Can dreams bring us news from other places, information from the future, or insights into other people's minds? Many people feel instinctively that they can, and telepathic dreaming has even been demonstrated clinically. In a famous experiment at the Maimonides Hospital in Brooklyn, New York, some volunteers concentrated on a selection of target pictures while others slept. When woken during periods of REM sleep, the sleepers reported a statistically significant number of dreams clearly influenced by the images.

Another well-known aspect of dreams is precognition – clairvoyant knowledge of future events, by which people have dreamed of impending disasters, including the sinking of the Titanic in 1912 and the Japanese attack on Pearl Harbor in 1941. Science has no explanation for this apparent ability to see into the future, but there are many well-documented cases based on reliable testimony.

Doom-laden dreams sometimes leave us with a general sense of foreboding. Later, we may become aware that the dream was a portent of catastrophe.

As a simple experiment in dream clairvoyance, try dreaming race horse winners. The less you know about racing, the better, because that way your rational mind is less likely to interfere and confuse matters. American psychologist Thelma Moss reports a case of a woman who dreamed up to four winners a week for four months, and there are many other proven examples. One curious proviso seems to be that the money so gained should be used for charitable purposes. Several dreamers have reported the loss of their ability if they spend their winnings on themselves.

Dreaming Race Winners

Dream Exercise 1

A good way to test precognitive dreaming is to try to predict the winner of a horse race. Of course, there is no need to place bets in order to follow this exercise. It is based on the system of elimination developed by an English retired engineer and public servant, Charles Horwood.

1 Pick a race a week ahead, give each runner a number and divide the runners randomly into two lists. Before going to bed, read the lists and think about the names and numbers. Put one list on the left side of the bed, and the other on the right.

2 In the morning, try to remember if your dreams suggested or contained a name or a number. Ask, too, whether "left" or "right" were emphasized in any dream, indicating which list might contain a winner. Make a note of your conclusions.

3 On the next night, redistribute the runners randomly into two new lists, keeping the same number for each horse. Repeat steps 1 and 2, filing your successive lists together with your notes on the dreams you have had.

4 Repeat this process every night, progressively isolating a runner by identifying which horses are consistently in the chosen list. If you find that a name or number is strongly suggested or featured in a dream, there is no need to continue with the elimination process.

Contacting the Dream World

" Of scenes of Nature, fields and mountains,
Of skies so beauteous after a storm, and at night the moon so
unearthly bright,
… I dream, I dream, I dream. "
Walt Whitman

Imagine going to the theatre to watch an exciting play, but being shown to a bad seat, far away from the stage and behind a pillar. You have a limited, half-obscured view of the stage, and are able to take in the merest frustrating fragments of the action. You find that you can make no sense of the play. The next evening you return to the theatre; the play is different, but your seat is the same. Again, you catch only glimpses of the stage, and can absorb only fleeting and meaningless snatches of the play. After several days of this experience, you are tempted to give up, vowing never to visit the theatre again.

However, theatre-goers who have a better view of what is going on insist that their experiences have been worthwhile, telling you of the beauty and interest of what they have seen. Stimulated by these accounts, you decide one day to find a better seat in the auditorium, and are amazed at what you see.

In the same way, most of us catch only tantalizing, mystifying glimpses of our dreams. The first step toward understanding and appreciating them is to obtain a better seat in the nightly theatre of sleep. In this chapter, we explore the many different ways to gain a better view of our dreams, and experience them with the richness and clarity that Walt Whitman enjoyed.

Unlocking the Potential

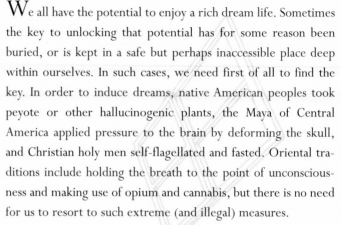

According to many Eastern traditions, dreams are insights of a "third eye" located in the forehead, just above and between the physical eyes. Touching this third eye with sandalwood oil or clear water before sleep is said to help it to see more clearly (see page 71).

We all have the potential to enjoy a rich dream life. Sometimes the key to unlocking that potential has for some reason been buried, or is kept in a safe but perhaps inaccessible place deep within ourselves. In such cases, we need first of all to find the key. In order to induce dreams, native American peoples took peyote or other hallucinogenic plants, the Maya of Central America applied pressure to the brain by deforming the skull, and Christian holy men self-flagellated and fasted. Oriental traditions include holding the breath to the point of unconsciousness and making use of opium and cannabis, but there is no need for us to resort to such extreme (and illegal) measures.

Dreams are essentially *visual* experiences, so honing our powers of visualization will bring us into closer contact with our inner selves. For many people, this means rediscovering an ability that has been lost since childhood. Try staring, without blinking, at an object or a scene. Close your eyes, but keep the image in your mind, remembering as much detail as you can; watch as it lingers in your imagination. If you find this difficult, choose a simple object such as a lighted candle, building up to more complex visualizations (see also page 54).

The next step is to show the mind that waking and dreaming visualizations are part of the same process. The following exercise is designed to foster this recognition by eroding the division between our waking and dreaming landscapes and allowing consciousness to flow more readily between the two.

Dissolving the Mental Wall

Dream Exercise 2

While we sleep, our dream selves rove unhindered in our creative inner world. This exercise, based on ancient techniques used in both Eastern and Western traditions, is a way to forge links between the waking world and the realm of dreams.

1 Imagine yourself looking out of a window at two different landscapes divided by a high wall. One landscape is the familiar world of everyday reality, but the second is the landscape of the dream world, where the laws of nature and logic are suspended.

2 Let your creative unconscious supply the details of the visualization. In the dream landscape, a road may transform itself into a river, houses may have eyes instead of windows, cars can fly through the air. Remember that neither landscape is more "real" than the other: both are creations of the imagination.

3 Allow the wall between the two landscapes to become insubstantial, like a grey mist drifting away in the wind, leaving the two landscapes in full communication with each other. See how artificial and flimsy the wall was.

4 Step in imagination into the scene in front of you, passing easily between the different landscapes, knowing that you are helping the waking and dreaming levels of your mind to become closer. When you feel ready to do so, open your eyes. Repeat the exercise as frequently as you wish, especially just before sleep.

*The four elements
– fire, air, earth and
water (left to right) –
are a good theme to
contemplate as a
starting point for
creative dreams.*

Dream Cue

*Devise a brief ritual
to perform before
sleep whenever you
want to set your
dreams free. It might
incorporate music,
chanting, gestures or
drumming. By
creating a special
"framework", and
concentrating the
mind on its task,
such devices can
facilitate dreaming.*

The ancient Greeks believed that the gods sent true dreams to us through gates of horn, while less meaningful dreams emerged through gates of ivory. Before sleeping, the dreamer would ask his or her chosen god for favourable dreams. You can perform a similar exercise, perhaps using the Greek gods to represent your own psychological energies. Conjure in your mind an image of the gates of horn, and choose one of the gods – perhaps Apollo, god of the arts, or Aphrodite, goddess of love. Imagine the deity sending you dreams of creative wisdom, inner harmony and well-being. Use golden or rainbow light, flowers or exotic fruits to symbolize these helpful and welcome dreams.

Shamanic traditions teach the need for an appropriate accompanying ritual involving smoke, considered a link between humankind and the great spirit. Incense is a safe, pleasant and practical way to provide smoke for a harmless ritual to arouse the creative imagination. Light an incense stick and hold it successively in each of the four points of the compass, representing the four elements: in your mind, link East with air, South with fire, West with water, and North with earth. Hold the stick high toward the sky (in shamanic traditions, representing the father) and then toward the earth (representing the mother). Devise your own visualization and form of words to accompany each of these movements, asking for dreams to be sent from the four directions, and from the sky above and the earth beneath.

Once you have established your potential for dreaming vividly, practise re-entering your dreams – that is, re-experiencing them during the day. One way to do this is to create in the mind a house for your dreams, which you can enter whenever you please, finding there the dreams you wish to recapture.

Building a House of Dreams

Dream Exercise 3

Allow a home for your dreams to emerge from your creative unconscious. Leave the
front door open, so that you can step inside whenever you wish, feeling in contact
with your dreams whether or not you are actively recalling them.

1 Close your eyes and ask your unconscious to show you a house of dreams. Do
not force things: if no images arise, open
your eyes and wait patiently for the image
to appear – it might take a day or two.

2 When the outside of the house is clear
in your mind's eye, open the front door and
go inside. Allow all the rooms and their fur-
nishings to emerge spontaneously, just as
you did the outside of the house.

3 Imagine that the house is occupied by the
memories of different kinds of dream.
Whether or not the house you imagined had

three stories, imagine that there are three
floors inside, each corresponding to a different level of dreaming. Climb up to see
what is on each of them.

4 Imagine that each room contains dream
memories. Wander through the
house, re-entering rooms and re-
visiting your dreams, prompting the unconscious to take
up the threads of unfin-
ished dreams, with a
view to completing
them and clarifying
their meaning.

Inventing a Dream Self

There is sometimes little relationship between dream events and the events of waking life. We may, for example, be experiencing stress and anxiety in our daily lives, yet find that we are enjoying euphoric dreams; at other times, success and happiness in daily life may seem to be undermined by sombre dreams.

This apparent incongruity may simply be a time-lag, reflecting a delay in the ability of the unconscious to absorb and respond to the happenings of the day. It may also indicate a lack of communication between the conscious and unconscious levels of our minds. More frequently, however, the discrepancy is caused by the unconscious mind's natural drive to compensate for the extremes of mood experienced in waking life. The unconscious level of the mind tends to be cautious in times of joy, and optimistic in the face of conscious disappointment: dreams are one of the tools it can use to maintain balance in our inner world.

By keeping us in contact with the unconscious mind in this way, dreams have the ability to illuminate areas shrouded in darkness, bringing harmony where there was discord, and making sure that we keep our equilibrium. In a real sense, they help us to face the ups and downs of everyday life.

We can actively seek this help, instead of waiting passively for it to come to us, by inventing a dream self to wander through our sleeping mind. Our dream self is like the imaginary companion we may have had as children. Such a dream helper can represent the person we aspire to be, or might be an unacknowledged aspect of our own self. The following exercise shows how we can liberate this adventurous hero of the unconscious – this Ulysses on the sea of sleep.

Dream Cue

Create an idealized version of your waking self, with all the physical and psychological attributes you would like to have. Contemplating and identifying with this perfect self before sleep will help you to develop a more positive self-image.

Setting Your Dream Self Free

Dream Exercise 4

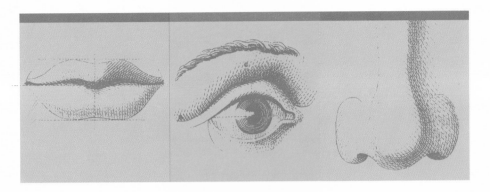

Try conjuring up a dream self, sending him or her into the dream world to act as your ambassador and carry out missions on your behalf.

1 Sit comfortably, close your eyes, and imagine that you are in front of a mirror. Allow the image of your reflection to build up as completely as possible, observing your face, hair and clothes just as you would in a real mirror.

2 Dissolve the mirror, leaving your image as if real and three-dimensional. Tell yourself that this is your dream body, a part of yourself that can penetrate deep into the unconscious.

3 Tell your dream body to travel tonight to the dream place you have chosen, to find the answer to a current problem, or to explore elusive areas of yourself – perhaps peace, happiness or self-confidence. Watch as your dream body willingly accepts your instructions, nodding and smiling.

4 See the image of yourself become once more an image in a mirror, then watch both image and mirror fading until you are securely back in the real world. When you feel ready, open your eyes to set your dream self free.

Remembering Your Dreams

Given that we all dream more or less the same amount, it is surprising how many people claim never to dream, or find that even their most gripping dreams vanish without trace when they wake up. This frustrating failure to remember dreams can be remedied with a little work. Some people find this task easier than others, but with proper training and dedication, we can all learn to recall far more of our nightly adventures.

The main reason we forget our dreams is simply that we do not regard them as important enough. Compared with other cultures and times, the modern Western lifestyle fails to recognize the power of dreams. It would be inconceivable for an Inuit or a Xhosa to say that he or she never dreamed, or that he always forgot his dreams. As a child, he would have learned of their importance, especially as a way to get closer to the spirit world. Most Westerners, by contrast, are brought up to believe that dreams serve no real purpose, and should not be taken seriously.

The transfer of material from the unconscious world of sleep to conscious, waking life is a delicate process. It can easily be disrupted by a conscious mind that refuses to acknowledge that the exercise is worthwhile. As soon as we start *wanting* to remember our dreams, we are on the road to succeeding.

Another psychological obstacle to remembering our dreams is that we may have been conditioned to repress them. Repression is a natural defence mechanism, protecting us against memories, desires or fears too painful or disturbing to be allowed into consciousness. Such material may be linked to early traumas or to thoughts and behaviour that we have been taught make us bad or unloved. It may relate to "unacceptable" drives such as sex, or to idealistic hopes and ambitions that we once had but have now had to admit will never come to fruition.

Any or all of these factors can emerge in dreams, only to be shut out by the mind at the moment of waking. If we can bring this material into consciousness, we may be able to learn much from it. A great deal of it is harmless and natural (it was erroneously labelled bad by others before we were old enough to judge for ourselves); the residue needs to be acknowledged and laid to rest.

Negative attitudes toward the activity of dreaming itself can also impede recall. Perhaps you have a conscious belief that dreamless sleep is more restful and relaxing, perhaps you become unsettled by the loss of control apparent in dreams, or feel somehow that we are not meant to remember them. There may be deep-seated unconscious reasons why you forget what you have dreamed: perhaps you dislike your dream self; maybe you fear the power of unpleasant dreams. You might feel simply that it is fanciful or self-indulgent to be interested in dreams, or that paying too much attention to them may render you less effective in waking life.

The first step to *working with your dreams is to improve your ability to remember them.*

Ask yourself what you really feel about dreaming. If you find negative attitudes, make an effort to re-assess and change them. Help the unconscious to get the message by frequently repeating positive affirmations. Tell yourself that your dreams are helpful, and that you will begin to remember them; make an effort to welcome what your dreams can teach you about yourself, and keep in mind the power of dreams to help you to become a more fulfilled and effective human being.

Such affirmations, delivered with confidence, are particularly helpful last thing at night. The unconscious is immediately aware of any doubt in our conscious minds, and all too often responds to this uncertainty rather than to the message. Sincerely believe that you can remember your dreams, and you will find that your dream memory becomes far more accurate.

However, dream memories are often distorted by the conscious mind. The mind recalls dream details, but changes them, often without realizing it, to avoid anything that it considers unwelcome. We progressively forget or alter some of the most revealing aspects of our dreams as time elapses after our initial recall, so we need to record our dreams, without censorship of any kind, as soon as possible after waking.

To supplement the conscious breaking down of impediments to dream recall, there are a number of techniques to enhance our ability to remember our dreams. Many of them have been used for centuries by the great spiritual and mystical traditions. Whether or not you believe in the theories behind them, the important thing to bear in mind is that these ancient techniques do actually work.

A nightly review of the day's events, starting with the dream memories of the previous night, greatly improves recall generally. Watch for links and associations between dream memories and the day's activities, building up the connections between the dream world and the real world to arrive at a fuller picture of both sides of your life.

Dream Cue

Ponder during the day the previous night's dreams, and then before you sleep that night try to make imaginative connections between those dreams and the day's events (as in the case study opposite). By weaving dreaming and waking episodes in this way, you can gain valuable insights into your preoccupations.

The Grail and the Balloon

Case Study 1

The young, ambitious business executive who had this dream found an ingenious way to weave it into the events of the next day, cleverly adapting its imagery to help ideas and memories flow between waking and sleeping life.

" I dreamed of two men in period costume, duelling with swords. The loser (the hero of my dream) had his head cut off. I knew that it was a dream, and that he would be resurrected when the dream ended, like an actor after the final curtain. Later, in waking life, I drove to work and realized that my old car is a 'period piece', like the costumes in the dream. At work, I had a disagreement — a 'duel with words' with my boss — and felt that he 'cut my head off'. "

" In the afternoon, the swords in the dream reminded me of King Arthur's sword Excalibur, and of the search for the Holy Grail. Excalibur has a hilt like a cross, but in the dream the period was different and the swords had basket hilts. 'Basket' made me think of a balloon with a basket. Later, my boss apologized for the morning. I felt that 'resurrection' can happen even before the 'final curtain'.

" Before bed, I mentally placed the day's good events into the Holy Grail, and the bad into the basket under the balloon. I released the balloon, and it vanished into the night sky, taking the day's problems away, and leaving me with only the good things. "

Techniques of Recall

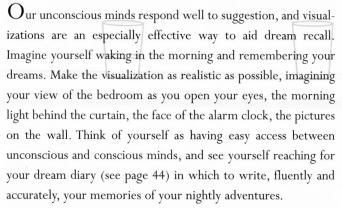

Our unconscious minds respond well to suggestion, and visual-izations are an especially effective way to aid dream recall. Imagine yourself waking in the morning and remembering your dreams. Make the visualization as realistic as possible, imagining your view of the bedroom as you open your eyes, the morning light behind the curtain, the face of the alarm clock, the pictures on the wall. Think of yourself as having easy access between unconscious and conscious minds, and see yourself reaching for your dream diary (see page 44) in which to write, fluently and accurately, your memories of your nightly adventures.

Like the dreamer in the previous case study (page 41), try to develop a sense of continuity between waking and sleeping, so that your consciousness flows unbrokenly from one to the other and back again. The process can be helped by drinking half a glass of water before sleep, placing the glass on the bedside table, and imagining yourself aware of it all night. See yourself drinking the rest in the morning. When morning comes, remember the details of your earlier visualization as you finish the water.

All methods for dream recall require a little time and patience. No technique is likely to work if you keep changing from one to another. Not only would this give the techniques little chance to become effective, but it would also inform the unconscious that you have little faith in any of them. As a result, the inner self may well fail to take them seriously.

Your ability to remember dreams is closely related to your ability to remember in general. The exercise opposite is a simple but effective way to improve your powers of memory in daily life, and therefore to help recapture your dreams.

Kim's Game

Dream Exercise 5

A valuable exercise for improving recall is "Kim's Game", an ancient Eastern practice described by Rudyard Kipling in his novel *Kim*. Whether or not it fulfils its reputed aim of helping to develop psychic powers, it certainly stretches the memory, and may assist dream recall.

1 Get a friend to place 10 objects on a tray. Look at them for 10 seconds, then write down as many of the objects as you can remember. Try if possible to remember them visually rather than by name.

2 As you become more skilled at the game, change the objects and increase their number, increasing the time allowance too by one second for each object added. Then, gradually shorten the length of time available.

3 After you have played the game a number of times, notice which kinds of objects you find easy to remember and which are more difficult. Do shape, colour or function affect recall? How can you ensure greater success with the difficult objects next time?

4 You may notice that objects that are useful or have pleasant associations are more readily recalled, indicating a need to pay extra attention to more neutral types of objects.

Keeping a Dream Diary

Whatever methods you use to help you to remember your dreams, a dream diary is essential. Keep a pen and notebook by your pillow, and write in it as soon as you wake each morning. Make as little other physical movement as possible – even turning over in bed can banish dream memories. Don't delay your writing until later: even the most vivid dreams quickly fade or become distorted in detail.

There are many different ways of keeping a dream diary. Some writers suggest having separate columns for events, characters, colours and emotions, but categorizing memories during recall can be another way of losing them. The best method is to write down the dream, and then analyze and categorize it at your leisure. Write your dreams on the left-hand page of the book, and keep the right-hand blank for interpretations, comments, sketches and subsequent analysis.

Make sure that each entry is dated, and that as much detail as possible is recorded – as you piece together an interpretation, it is sometimes the most apparently insignificant aspects of a dream that turn out to be most revealing. Always write in the present tense: try to re-live the dream as you record it, and make a careful note of your emotions. On the facing page is a typical entry from a dream diary.

" *I am in a toy store, surrounded by old-fashioned toys, rather like a
Victorian toy museum. I decide to buy a box of large wooden soldiers with red
coats, but when I take them to the counter to pay, the assistant tells me that
they are not for sale. His face is in shadow, but I notice his black clothes, and
his triangular wing collar. Instead of the soldiers, he asks me to choose a book
from a large bookshelf which I have not previously noticed.* "

" *Feeling disappointed, I take a book at random, and turn the pages.
It is full of pictures, and suddenly I am a small child again, sitting at
the green kitchen table in our old home, and looking at a child's picture
book. There is a picture of the window of a toy store, and in the centre there is
a box of wooden soldiers. The assistant, stiff and wooden, in his black clothes
and wing collar, is in the middle of the box. I feel angry, as if he has
tricked me, and think, 'He hasn't even bothered to put on his uniform'.* "

Sketching Dreams

Dream Exercise 6

Whatever your artistic ability, capturing the visual "feel" of a dream will help you to
pin down important details, the meaning of which may only become clear much later.

1 Quick doodles in your dream diary
help you to describe and remember your
dreams, but for more detailed drawings
you should keep a separate sketch book.

2 Artistic skill is not important in the
dream sketch book: what really matters
is that you sincerely attempt to convey the
emotional feel and atmosphere of the
dream. The very process of sketching your
dreams prompts further dream recall, and
enables the unconscious to provide associations and reveal symbols that aid dream
interpretation.

*In dreams, **blue** – the colour
of the sky – often symbolizes
intellect, tranquillity and
contemplation.*

***Green** is the colour of nature
and the senses, but also,
depending upon context, envy
or decay.*

***White** has connotations
of purity and virginity, but
also of mourning and the
desire for transcendence.*

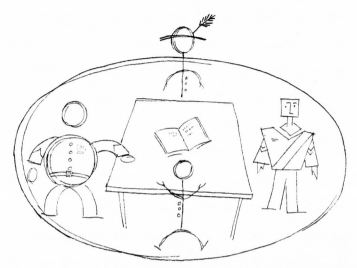

3 Try sketching your dreams in both representational and abstract ways. As well as human figures, pay particular attention to geometrical shapes (the cross, circle, triangle, square) and to the elements, the moon, and the other heavenly bodies whenever they occur. Represent the dream sometimes as a mandala (concentric diagram for meditation), with the

theme in the centre and the associations arising from it arranged all around. Work spontaneously and intuitively, without censorship; don't allow the conscious mind to interfere.

4 Colours play an important role in dreams, and should be carefully noted in the sketchbook. Each colour has its own symbolism, as shown below.

Red *is the symbol of energy, life and aggression: the colour of blood and anger.*

Gold *represents majesty and divinity, as well as the sun and masculinity.*

Black *is death, but also resurrection and the darkness of the unconscious.*

Violet *is the colour of the mystical union of opposites (blue and red).*

Making Connections

If life can be pictured as a tapestry of feelings, ideas, activities and people, then our dreams are like embroidered golden threads, stitched deep into the fabric of our past, present and future, highlighting our innermost concerns. The diary and sketchbook in which you log your dreams can indicate the repeating patterns, helping you to develop a sense of how your dream life can sometimes serve as a coherent commentary on your waking life, by picking out key motifs.

Personal possessions and *obsessions often loom large in our dreams, revealing the architecture of our inner lives.*

Look for links between dreams and real events, both recent and from the distant past. In particular, search your dream diary for recurring dreams, whose repetitive themes or images can reveal deep concerns which the dreamer needs to address squarely. Recurring dreams often indicate a need for the dreamer to express certain aspects of his or her personality; they can also reveal entirely hidden parts of the dreamer's inner life.

As you accumulate dreams in your diary, you will start to discern certain images, incidents, characters, places and even emotions building slowly to make a complete picture of your psychic identity. At first, the outlines may be sketchy; but once you have started to trace the connections, it is worth trying to flesh out the portrait, using a simple, restful ritual (see opposite) to nudge your sleeping mind in a particular direction.

Building a Dream Temple

Dream Exercise 7

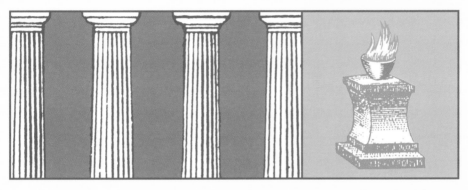

This exercise, designed to induce dreams of particular subjects, is derived from the ancient Greek practice of sleeping in holy places to ask for divine guidance.

1 As you lie in bed waiting for sleep, imagine that you are in the centre of a Greek temple, with four white pillars. Place a stone altar in front of one of the pillars.

2 Visualize upon the altar any objects or symbols that carry special meaning for you: images of loved ones; treasured possessions; significant books or pictures; or resonant images that have recurred in your dreams. Place candles at the centre and at each end of the altar.

3 The space around you is now illuminated by soft, flickering candlelight. The details

of the temple outside the pillars fade into the shadows, but you can make out statues of gods and goddesses in the half-light.

4 In front of the altar there is a low wooden bed. Move forward, bow to the altar and lie down on the bed.

5 Gaze at the objects on the altar by your side, and drift toward sleep, holding around you an awareness of the temple and its subtle dream magic.

Contacting the Unconscious

As you work to develop stronger dream skills, bear in mind that the unconscious does not learn in the same way as the conscious mind. The latter is usually rational, logical and linear; it searches for patterns and relationships, thrives on consistency and pre-dictability, thinks primarily in terms of words, and can readily test itself on what it has learned. By contrast, the unconscious appears to follow no rules, to be stubborn and wilful, and to make progress in a frustratingly inconsistent and unpredictable way. It sometimes obstinately refuses to cooperate: we all know how our minds can lay an anxiety to rest, while our emotions, prompted by the unconscious, continue to fret.

It would be unrealistic to expect the unconscious to respond like the conscious mind. Even after a long period of intense effort, it may apparently fail to get the message you are trying to convey, only to reward you when you least expect it with the result that you have been seeking. It is important to be patient, and not to waver in your belief that the unconscious will respond.

The unconscious does, however, resemble the conscious mind in that it responds well to praise. You must befriend it, letting it know how much you value it. Reward it verbally and with warm feelings for the dreams it gives you, and make sure you thank it for any improvement in your dream life. Ask what further help you can give to it, and wait in silence for the answers it provides. Never regard actions of this kind as fanciful. They are an effective way of self-integration, and produce a

Contemplating archetypal themes in literature, such as the story of desire and enthralment recounted by Keats in his poem "La Belle Dame Sans Merci", can bring benefits to our dream lives.

range of psychological benefits as well as improvements in dreaming.

The best way to approach the unconscious is through simplicity and repetition. Give it instructions that are clear and unambiguous, such as "I am going to remember my dreams" or "I am going to fly in my dreams." Repeat them frequently.

Listen to music which you feel echoes or represents the dream mood you wish to experience; read romantic or mystical poetry, visualizing its sym-

bols and pondering the deep metaphors involved. Watch and listen as your mind learns how to absorb impressions, and resist the temptation to reduce these impressions to the level of rational, linear thought by expressing them as words.

It may be helpful to think of the unconscious as the source of your psychological life, and to see the conscious mind as a kind of overlay, placed over it by learning and experience. The more rigid and inflexible the conscious mind becomes, the more thoroughly it prevents the energy of the unconscious from emerging into awareness.

We can also encourage the different aspects of the mind to work in unison by employing a simple visual metaphor. Visualize the conscious mind as a staid, puritanical doorkeeper holding closed the door through which the unconscious is vainly trying to enter. Now imagine the conscious mind opening the door and greeting the unconscious as a long-lost brother or sister, and watch as the two aspects of the mind agree that they both have much to learn from each other. Feel certain that from now on, they will work together in harmony.

Dream Cue

As you fall asleep, visualize your unconscious as a separate being in the room with you. What journeys would you like it to embark on tonight?

The Art of Dream Control

" People can learn to control their dreams in a way that is helpful to them ... they can provide themselves with the feed-back information to shape their dreams to their own benefit. "
Patricia Garfield

In her extensive studies of dreams and dreamers, Patricia Garfield discovered not only that the desire to control dream content is virtually universal, but that techniques for doing so have been known and practised from ancient times and across many cultures. No matter when or where they have been adopted, these techniques show many similar features, a fact that in itself testifies to their effectiveness.

It may seem surprising to learn that we can control the activities of our sleeping minds, but we have already seen that we can greatly enhance our ability to remember our dreams. The next step is to influence them to go the way we want. As well as asking dreams to provide us with fascinating adventures and wonderful imagery, we can stimulate dreams that increase our self-knowledge, and show the way to inner harmony.

If we learn how to control the content of our dreams, we immediately make them more relevant to our lives. We can ask them to help us solve specific problems and cross-examine them to bring out their meaning. We can make our dreams more enjoyable and more poetic. In effect, we can become authors not of confusing and dull guide books, but of travelogues illustrated by pictures of the most beautiful scenery, and illuminated on every page by vivid writing.

Developing Dream Skills

Our minds are constantly at work imagining all manner of activities. As we set out for a trip to the coast, for example, we anticipate what the beach will look like, how the sea will sound as it laps across the shore, the tang of salt in the air. We arrange to meet a friend, and fleetingly see ourselves greeting him or her in the agreed place. By honing this ability to visualize, we can practise a vital dreaming skill.

As an initial step toward effective visualization, make the most of vision itself. All too often, we "see" our surroundings without truly "looking" at them. Spend time in natural surroundings, paying special attention to the forms, colours and patterns of nature. In cities, note the curve of the street and the rhythms of architecture; indoors, see how light and shadow shape a room, noticing the texture and colour of furniture, walls and fabrics.

Make a special effort to observe and absorb art, the fruit of the creative unconscious. The great visual artists – from Hieronymus Bosch, via Michelangelo, Monet and Van Gogh, to Giorgio de Chirico and Mark Rothko – have drawn on the deepest recesses of their imagination to create haunting images of universal significance. Tarot cards, native American and Australian aboriginal art and Indian or Tibetan mandalas can supply the same inspiration.

If we look at these images, hold them in the mind and embrace their mystery, they become part of our unconscious. Like a computer operated to manipulate raw data, the unconscious can change them. The next exercise is designed to extend our visualization skills – vital tools if we are to control our dreams.

The Tarot, a potent symbolic system, supplies a range of images for meditation. In the Star, for example, a maiden pours from two pitchers, an action that could represent ambiguity or division.

Morphing the Apple

Dream Exercise 8

In dreams, objects sometimes transform themselves in complex and bizarre ways that can reveal a symbolic meaning. This exercise is designed to help the visual imagination to become more nimble, breaking down the tyranny of fixed forms.

1 Focus on a red apple, visualize it carefully and then, holding its image clearly in your mind, mentally change its colour from red to green and back again. Do this several times.

2 Now visualize the apple decaying, becoming wizened and finally rotten. Next, reverse the process and watch as the apple grows younger again. See it become fresh again and go back through its stages of growth until it ends up as a bud. Bring the apple back to its original state, visiting all the stages again. Open your eyes and see how close your visualization remains to the original.

3 Close your eyes and visualize the apple again. This time, transform it into an orange, the orange into a pear and back into an apple. Now change it by stages into a tennis ball and then a crystal ball.

4 Try a similar exercise with the human face and body, changing the image from youth to age, male to female. Visualize changes of costume and expression.

5 Say to yourself that the place where images "exist" is as much in your mind as in the outside world. Feel confident in your ability to control and transform what you see in dreams.

Dreams of Flight

The urge to rise into the air is one of the central themes of human fantasy. In mythology and legend, the power of flight is reserved for the gods and other supernatural beings, such as angels and fairies, cherubs and seraphs. Pegasus the winged horse, Mercury the winged messenger and the flying carpet of Arabian legend are all symbols of a fascination that keeps mankind always looking upward in hope and longing. Even the modern cartoon character Superman, with his extraordinary powers of flight, taps into this primeval yearning to leave earthly concerns behind and reach for the skies.

Dream Cue

Next time you take an aeroplane journey, close your eyes and imagine that the rest of the aircraft has disappeared. Drift off into a light sleep, as you feel yourself soaring across the sky. If you then have a flying dream, you may awake to find yourself profoundly refreshed or even exhilarated.

It is partly because of these deep aspirations that flying is one of the most exciting dream experiences open to us. For most people, taking to the air in dreams produces a sense of freedom and release from normal physical, cultural and emotional constraints. To escape from gravity in dreams is one way to escape from all the daily concerns that "weigh us down" spiritually. According to some commentators, dreams of flight are closely related to psychic out-of-body experiences, in which the soul or spirit seems to "float free" of the physical body.

Some dreamers report that flying dreams leave them with a sense of elation that affects the way they feel about themselves and the world for long afterward. Perhaps these dreams are intended to remind us of our almost infinite spiritual and psychological potential. As if to confirm this, it is very rare for people – even those with a terror of heights or of travelling by air – to experience fear during flying dreams; indeed, the dream may be intended to reassure the dreamer that these terrors are not real. We can ask for dreams of flight without fear.

Learning to Fly

Dream Exercise 9

To overcome our conscious awareness that we cannot fly, and so encourage
flying dreams, this visualization exercise starts off by identifying with animals
and objects that can free themselves from gravity.

1 During the day, make a point of looking for flying objects. Follow the flight of birds with your eyes; tell yourself that you too can fly, in the same way, in dreams.

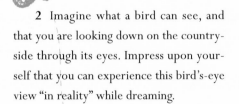

2 Imagine what a bird can see, and that you are looking down on the country-side through its eyes. Impress upon yourself that you can experience this bird's-eye view "in reality" while dreaming.

3 Release a feather, a petal, a flying seed, a balloon or a kite into the wind, and follow its progress. Remind yourself that if you can send such items into the air in this world, you can send yourself there in the dream world.

4 Imagine your body becoming lighter, feeling less and less of your weight being taken by the ground under your feet. Tell yourself that when dreaming your body will be able to rise effortlessly into the air.

5 Before going to sleep, remember all the exercises that you have done during the day. As you drift off to sleep, vow to take these experiences with you, and to relive them in your dreams.

Encouraging Creative Dreams

Although many people would claim that they have no real creative outlet in their waking lives, everyone experiences rich creativity in their dreams. Our imagination, released from the mundane concerns of waking hours, runs free: we enter surreal landscapes or strange, impossible buildings; we transform familiar faces and places; we even invent entirely new characters or become different people ourselves.

Any creative act typically involves four stages: the recognition that a particular theme has creative potential or that a problem requires a creative solution; a period of incubation, during which the unconscious ponders upon this initial stimulus; a moment of illumination, when the unconscious introduces a creative idea into consciousness; and finally a process of verification, during which the idea is tested, expressed or implemented. Dreams are particularly helpful in the second and third stages. We can harness our dreaming minds to come up with the initial creative spark, incubate it and show it to our conscious minds.

In this way, dreams have supplied authors with plots and artists with images, while composers have literally "dreamed up" melodies. Whether these dreams build on ideas that have been in the conscious mind before sleeping, or whether they introduce themes stored in the unconscious, the result is inspiration.

Of all the stories of inspiration from the dream world, one of the best-known examples is that of the 19th-century Scottish writer Robert Louis Stevenson, who claimed that half his work was "done for me while ... asleep". Stevenson wanted to write a novel exploring the idea that we all have our good and bad sides. After two days "wracking my brains for a plot," the story of what

Dream Cue

Spend some time in bed before sleep looking carefully at a colour reproduction of a painting – perhaps one painted in rich detail (such as a Vermeer), or in a more suggestive, shadowy style (such as a Rembrandt). Imagine details that are outside the frame, or behind walls, or obscured by shadow. In the morning, see if you can remember from your dreams any features that you visualized in the painting.

was to become *The Strange Case of Dr Jekyll and Mr Hyde* came to him in the night: "I dreamed the scene at the window, and a scene afterwards … in which Hyde, pursued for some crime, took the powder and underwent the change."

The English novelist Graham Greene, too, found that he could use dreams to enhance his creativity, stating, "I imagine all authors have found the same aid from the unconscious." The idea of *The Honorary Consul* came to him in a dream, and another dream filled a nagging gap in the narrative of *A Burnt-Out Case*. In the latter example, he actually dreamed that he was one of his own characters, revealing a way through what had become a dead end in the plot.

Beethoven and Wagner are among many composers who acknowledged their debt to dreams. In our own time, a dream supplied Paul McCartney with the melody for the Beatles' hit *Yesterday*: "I just woke up one morning and … I'd got this little song in my head. I found my way to the piano, sleepily, and I found the chords that it seemed to be. And I thought, it can't have just come to me in a dream – it doesn't happen, does it?"

In successful art, especially painting and creative writing, it is the element of surprise – of defying cliché – that holds the onlooker's or reader's attention. Surrealism, in which everyday expectations are blatantly overturned, is the extreme example of this approach. But even in more realistic genres, it is the unexpected that delivers the necessary frisson, and in this respect dreams may provide not only a rich source of subject matter, but also the "stretching exercises" that help the imagination to become more supple – and more responsive to offbeat moods and happenings.

Inspiration from dreams *can help us to carry out an essential task of creativity: playing with our ideas, trying them for size and rearranging them until they make a coherent whole.*

Sleeping on Problems

While we sleep, the mind continues to work, processing information, storing memories, sometimes untying even the knottiest intellectual, emotional or moral problems. Unencumbered by the conventions of the conscious mind, the unconscious is free to take an unorthodox approach that can provide the very breakthrough that we have been racking our brains for.

Dream Cue

Draw or paint a picture before sleep, deliberately leaving it incomplete. Ask your dream to supply the missing details. If they do not appear in a dream, they may well spring to mind when you look at the unfinished picture in the morning.

We have all spent hours pondering an apparently insoluble question, only to wake up with the answer. Overnight, the sleeping brain has incubated the problem, analyzing it and bringing the solution into consciousness as we awake. One way to test this process, at a superficial level, is to ask a friend to give you a riddle, puzzle or anagram. If you cannot solve it by your conscious efforts, hand it over to your unconscious.

Asking your unconscious for help is a matter of holding the problem in your mind before going to sleep, feeling relaxed and confident in the knowledge that *you* have no need to worry about the solution during the night: your sleeping mind will do all the work, and may reveal the answer in the morning, either as a fully-formed reply or buried in a dream.

When you wake up, you may find that you simply "know" the solution. If not, search for it in your dreams, where it could appear symbolically, or as a visual or verbal pun, which may need further interpretation. You can even suggest appropriate symbolism to your dreaming mind, as in the following exercise.

Posing a Visual Question

Dream Exercise 10

This exercise uses objects to symbolize aspects of a problem, leaving the
unconscious free to explore every avenue for an answer.

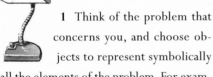

1 Think of the problem that concerns you, and choose objects to represent symbolically all the elements of the problem. For example, if the problem concerns colleagues at work, a large bottle might stand for a pompous and over-bearing boss, a toy lion for a courageous ally, a calculator for an accountant. If you have a chess set, try using the board and its pieces to represent the problem. For example, for a family problem, you might use the king and queen to represent mother and father, pawns for children, a castle (rook) for the children's school, bishops for teachers, and knights for loyal friends.

2 Arrange the items to represent the problem awaiting solution – perhaps in mutually exclusive power groups, scattered in haphazard administrative chaos, or supine to represent powerlessness.

3 Survey the arrangement, and tell yourself to dream about the problem during the night. The solution could appear in a number of forms, presenting itself in terms of the people concerned, the symbols you have been using, or in some other way.

4 Be prepared to repeat the exercise for several nights, giving your unconscious time to mull over the problem.

Arranging a Dream Rendezvous

One way to test our ability to control our dreams is to arrange to meet someone else in them, and to share the same dream. This may seem like a wildly improbable project, yet people who are emotionally close to each other can have very similar dreams. This might be because they share many of the waking experiences that provide the dreaming mind with its subject matter, but sometimes the shared dream is quite unexpected in content and can be corroborated by comparing specific details.

Some Western mystical fraternities and Eastern spiritual traditions actively encourage their members to share their dreams as part of the process of realizing their true nature. The belief is that although the dream body is usually left to wander aimlessly in the dream world, without direction or purpose, it can help with this realization. One way to remedy the dream body's habitual aimlessness is to give it specific tasks, such as meeting a friend.

Oliver Fox, an English researcher and writer, agreed with two friends to meet on a nearby green in their dreams. That night Fox dreamed that he met one of his friends there, but not the other. The following day the friend who had been present recounted a similar dream, while the absent friend could not remember dreaming at all.

It is worth persisting with dream sharing, even if you have no success initially. If you do succeed, it is fascinating to discuss the differences and similarities with your friend or partner.

Dream Cue

If you visit an especially beautiful or impressive place with a friend, promise to meet up again there in your dreams. This works especially well if you have time to become steeped in the history and atmosphere of the place.

Meeting in Sleep

Dream Exercise 11

Work with a partner, close friend or relative who is interested in the attempt, and who is at least open-minded as to its chances of success. People who have a close emotional bond are more likely to be successful in this undertaking than casual acquaintances.

1 Sit or lie down comfortably with your chosen partner. Decide together on a meeting place which has pleasant, but not over-intense, emotional associations for you both. Spend time "tuning in" to each other, talking about the chosen place, discussing your shared memories and enjoying feelings of mutual harmony.

2 When the mood is right, visualize with your partner the place that you want to visit. Describe the scene to each other; as you listen, enter the scene in your imagination, filling in the details and telling each other what you see.

3 After several of these sessions, decide to meet there on a particular night at a set time, and feel confident that you will do so. Make your arrangements very detailed, and rehearse them inwardly as frequently as possible, especially before sleep.

4 In the morning, make a point of telling each other your dreams as soon as you can. Compare your dreams carefully, and look for correspondences.

5 Be patient, and be prepared to try the experiment many times. Defeatism and scepticism are major obstacles to success.

Lucid Dreams

No matter how bizarre or unusual our dream adventures, we seldom realize at the time that they are, in fact, dreams, because to the sleeping mind the dream world is as real as waking reality. There are, however, ways to dream while enjoying full consciousness. In rare cases we can even retain consciousness during dreamless sleep, an experience akin to profound levels of meditation.

Dreams in which we have full awareness are known as lucid dreams, a term coined in 1913 by the Dutch physician Frederick Van Eeden, a prolific lucid dreamer. If we learn how to recognize that we are dreaming, we can take control of our dreams, create a dream environment of our choice and, in some cases, "travel" to actual locations to carry out a pre-arranged mission.

Tibetan Buddhism teaches that lucid dreams are a way of preparing to exercise control in the afterlife – an environment similar to the dream world. In this way, we can eventually free ourselves from the illusory cycle of life and death. Indeed,

Tibetan Buddhists maintain that the prime purpose of dreaming is to give us a nightly opportunity to gain this control.

The American psychologist Charles Tart suggests that we use the freedom available in lucid dreams to seek or create a wise man or woman from whom we can ask advice on our psychological or spiritual growth. Such a creation might be a personalization of our own unconscious wisdom, but he or she may bring information charged with a truth and profundity unavailable to the conscious mind.

Western therapists and counsellors have long taught that lucid dreaming is an essential skill on the path to inner development. As well as being an important way to explore the true nature of consciousness, the ability to control the content of a dream is good mental discipline – an exercise of will that can strengthen our understanding of an aspect of ourselves that still defies modern scientific understanding. Moreover, lucid dreaming is a major step toward enabling consciousness to leave the body in a so-called "out-of-body experience" (OBE). In lucid dreams, consciousness wanders in the "astral realms"– worlds created by thought and imagination. In OBEs, by contrast, this consciousness often remains on the earthly plane and is aware of physical reality, including very often the presence of its owner's body in the room. The line between an OBE and a lucid dream, however, is often blurred.

***The power of choice** – the right fork in the road, rather than the left – is what makes lucid dreaming so exhilarating. Not only is the dreamer conscious of the ability to shape the dream as desired: he or she also gains a greatly heightened sensual awareness.*

The Lucid Dream Experience

The experience of lucid dreaming is unmistakable and unforgettable. While remaining asleep, the dreamer approaches waking consciousness and suddenly becomes aware of his or her ability to shape the dream as desired. The dream takes on the sharp focus of waking life: sensitivity is heightened, colours become especially vivid and emotions assume a new intensity.

Full control of the dream, however, remains impossible. Dream events remain the preserve of the unconscious, which means that they remain unpredictable. The lucid dreamer may make the decision to visit a tropical island, but the actual scenery, and what happens on arrival, will have a life of their own.

A related phenomenon is false awakening, in which the dreamer rationalizes his or her emergence toward consciousness during a dream by forming the impression that he or she has actually woken up and is brushing teeth, getting dressed and having breakfast. On actually awakening, the dreamer may find it hard to believe that this experience was in fact unreal, and is astonished to find that he or she is still in bed.

Both lucid dreaming and false awakening indicate that it is possible to retain a considerable degree of consciousness while we dream, but lucid dreaming represents an almost complete meeting of the conscious and unconscious levels of the mind. We can consciously form an intention in the dream, deciding to visit a place or a person, to open a door or perform a particular action, but the unconscious will always determine the outcome.

Dream Cue

Take a fresh look at the world of nature, regarding it with the eyes of a child. Marvel at a bird in flight, and admire the shimmer of a fish's scales. Watch your dreams for enhanced visual content.

Among the Rooftops

Case Study 2

The dreamer is a young undergraduate student who has been practising techniques to induce lucid dreaming for some time. This is not her first lucid dream.

" One night I was dreaming of a small grey-stone town, with old-fashioned bow-fronted shops. I was riding an ancient bicycle with very flat tyres. I thought, 'Why am I not in my car?' and the realization came: 'I'm dreaming!' The effect was electrifying. Everything took on an extraordinary vibrancy, almost as if the dream had been in black and white before. I was exhilarated, and decided to fly. Totally unexpectedly I was plucked vertically into the air, then thrown onto my back. At roof level I caught hold of a chimney and held on. People below looked up puzzled, as if aware that something odd was happening, but unable to see me. Then the dream lost lucidity and turned into something about losing my way on a building site. But the experience was unforgettable. "

This dream contains many features of lucid dream experiences. The dreamer recognizes an anomaly (the bicycle), whereupon she realizes that she is dreaming, and the atmosphere changes. She takes control and decides to fly, but the dream determines how this happens. People in the dream seem aware that something is happening, yet are unaware of her. It is as if she is visiting a real town in her dream body. Then the dream becomes non-lucid — often it is as hard to retain lucidity as it is to achieve it in the first place.

Heightened Awareness

Dream Cue

Choose a familiar activity, such as swimming or walking or reading. Search your dream diary to see if you do the same in dreams. Try to persuade yourself that the next time you swim in a dream, you will have the power to swim where you please.

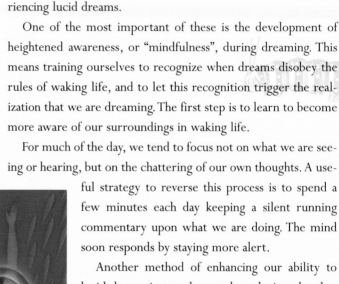

Some people are natural lucid dreamers; others rarely, if ever, have these spectacular dreams. Many gain the ability as a by-product of meditation practice, but there are several other techniques that we can all use to increase the likelihood of experiencing lucid dreams.

One of the most important of these is the development of heightened awareness, or "mindfulness", during dreaming. This means training ourselves to recognize when dreams disobey the rules of waking life, and to let this recognition trigger the realization that we are dreaming. The first step is to learn to become more aware of our surroundings in waking life.

For much of the day, we tend to focus not on what we are seeing or hearing, but on the chattering of our own thoughts. A useful strategy to reverse this process is to spend a few minutes each day keeping a silent running commentary upon what we are doing. The mind soon responds by staying more alert.

Another method of enhancing our ability to lucid-dream is to ask ourselves during the day, "How do I know that this isn't a dream?" Be as specific as possible with the answers, which will alert the mind to the differences of quality, sensation and emotion between waking and dreaming. When remembering dreams or looking through your dream diary, ask yourself, "Why didn't I recognize that this was a dream?" and instruct yourself that when similar dream experiences occur in the future, you will realize your true state of mind.

Painting the Imaginary Tree

Dream Exercise 12

By carrying out a visualization exercise just on the verge of sleep, we can increase the likelihood of lucid dreaming. This method, based on an Eastern meditation technique, is designed to stimulate and nourish our innermost creative powers.

1 Imagine that you are an artist painting a splendid tree standing on its own in a large open field. You study the tree in detail, taking in the shape of the branches and the spread of the green leaves overhead.

2 Look down at the canvas and examine your attempt. You are quite pleased with it, but it is not perfect: some of the branches are wrong, and you haven't yet captured the light shining through the foliage.

3 So get to your feet and walk around the tree, examining it from every angle. Look at the big gnarled roots, the deep fissures

of the bark, the hole in which a nesting bird has taken up residence.

4 Rise effortlessly into the air and look down on the tree as if you are that bird. Observe the tiny insects scurrying along the thin twigs at the top of the tree.

5 Return to your canvas and by an act of will change your painting so that it conforms to your new vision of the tree. Just as you can control your painting through willpower, so you can change the landscape. Decide that more trees will grow, and see them appear as if by magic.

Programming the Unconscious

By making repeated suggestions to yourself during the day that you will become lucid in your dreams, it is possible to program your unconscious – a process known as autosuggestion. Charles Tart recommends using the sentence, "Tonight I shall know that I am dreaming, and I shall awaken in the dream world." Repeat the vow several times very firmly as you are falling asleep.

Instructing your dream self to seek a mirror in your dreams, and trying to see your own reflection in it, can become a powerful catalyst for lucid dreaming, so long as you rehearse this cue sufficiently beforehand.

You can also imagine yourself back in a recent dream, only this time knowing that you are dreaming. If there is an object or event that features frequently in your dreams, such as a house or a carnival, use it as a signal: tell your waking mind that the next time it appears in dreams, you will realize that you are dreaming. You could also choose an activity that you regularly perform in dreams – perhaps driving a car or building a wall. Whatever object, event or activity you select, visualize it as often as possible during the day.

Another method is to create a cue for lucid dreaming. Instruct

your dream self to find a mirror and look into it, and promise yourself that you will know that you are dreaming when you see your reflection. This technique is especially effective, perhaps because it is an unusual dream experience: people rarely dream of seeing themselves in mirrors. If you frequently dream of water, tell yourself to go and look for your reflection in the surface.

To enhance our ability to realize that we are dreaming, we can also make use of an exercise based on the ancient Eastern belief that we see visions and dreams through a third eye, situated in the middle of the forehead (see opposite).

The Third Eye

Dream Exercise 13

By creating a waking equivalent of a lucid dream, this exercise will help you to stimulate lucidity during sleep.

1 Close your eyes and rest your concentration on the space behind your eyelids. Create a triangle there, with your eyes as the base and a point just above and between them as the apex.

2 Move the focus of your concentration up the sides of the triangle to the apex, which you now sense is a third eye. Allow the vision of a door to appear to this eye.

3 Watch as it opens to reveal the scene beyond. Step through the door and into the scene, knowing that you can return whenever you wish. Explore what you find – perhaps a landscape, a town, or a forest.

4 At the end of the exercise, walk back through the door, and look back to see it close and fade behind you. Re-establish the triangle with which you started the exercise, and shift the focus of your concentration from the third eye at the apex to your physical eyes at the base. You are now back in normal reality: open your eyes to see your familiar surroundings.

5 Before you go to sleep, run through the exercise again. See the door before you, and watch it open a little, then stop. Instruct your dreaming mind to open it fully and enter lucidly into the dream world beyond.

The Dedicated Dreamer

Shamanic traditions have their own greatly prized form of lucid dreaming, in which shamans take the opportunity to travel to the spirit world to meet tribal ancestors and legendary elders, learn songs of power, and find a spirit companion who will guide and teach the dreamer in waking life. Often the shaman undergoes long periods of solitude and intensive mind training in order to develop the necessary skills. A Mexican shaman, for example, said that "to learn to see, to learn to hear ... you must go into the wilderness alone ... such things are learned only in solitude".

Westerners, who are less patient and more convinced by the power of technology, sometimes make use of "dream machines" to monitor the onset of REM sleep. These machines use weak electrical impulses to tell sleepers that they are dreaming, without actually waking them. The theory is that the dreamer will continue with the dream, which now becomes lucid.

The results of working with dream machines are variable.

Some people find that with a little experimentation they work well, but it is debatable whether dream machines can prompt the quality of lucid dreaming that arises from appropriate mind training. They may provide a context for inner illumination, but they cannot provide the content.

Whatever techniques are used, patience is essential. Our culture has long neglected lucid dreaming, and we cannot expect to re-program our minds in a single session; but the exercise opposite is one method to extend waking consciousness into our sleeping hours.

On the Dream Highway

Dream Exercise 14

We have seen how to erode the barriers dividing waking life and dream life. Now we can explore ways to transfer our awareness between these worlds.

1 As you lie in bed waiting for sleep to come, imagine that you are standing on a footbridge over a busy road. Watch the oncoming traffic, and follow several vehicles with your eyes.

2 One car begins to slow down as it approaches. When it arrives below you, you find that you suddenly become the driver, watching the scenery flowing past. The road ahead is the road between waking and sleeping.

3 Remain watchful as you travel. Be aware of the sights, sounds and scents of the scenery through which you are passing.

Allow the vehicle to take you forward toward conscious sleep.

4 When you awake the following morning, recall the journey in as much detail as you can. Resolve that the next night you will take the same journey, but will remain conscious until you have travelled further along the road.

5 As you persist each night with the exercise, you should find that your consciousness (but not your wakefulness) will increasingly extend into your sleeping hours. This will make it easier to achieve lucid dreams.

In order to bring the sharp awareness of consciousness into our dream life, we need to learn a looser definition of reality, and come to believe that there is no great difference between seeing the real world and seeing the world of dreams. Shamanic traditions view some form of hardship as an essential aid to this sort of learning. An Inuit shaman told Arctic explorer Knud Rasmussen: "All true wisdom is only to be learned ... out in the great solitude ... Privation and suffering are the only things that can open the mind of man to those things that are hidden from others." Another said: "I have searched in the darkness, being silent in the great lonely stillness of the dark. So I became a [shaman] through visions and dreams and encounters with flying spirits." Cushioned as we are by the comforts of Western life, we have much to learn from such dedication.

Isolation from the throng of society can help dreamers to find the sense of detachment that intensifies the dream experience.

The shaman, like the Tibetan Buddhist, frequently links the trance state and lucid dreaming with death and the afterlife. Typically he or she undergoes torment in the dream world before being reborn in the waking world with magical powers — a pattern that appears to symbolize the dismantling of the domineering ego and the re-creation of the sufferer as a more liberated or enlightened being.

Many contemporary schools of thought echo this emphasis on setting aside the ego — but reject the shamanic belief that it is necessary to suffer in order to achieve this aim. By freeing ourselves from the selfish demands of the ego, we take an important step on the road to self-enlightenment. The exercise opposite suggests a gentle way of loosening the ego's grip, at the same time boosting our ability to control our consciousness.

Taking a Mental Self-portrait

Dream Exercise 15

This is a modern adaptation of a traditional technique for transferring
consciousness. The exercise aims to strengthen control over the imagination,
and hence encourage lucid dreaming.

1 Imagine that you are a photographer standing on a hillside, and about to take a picture across a valley of the scene on the opposite side. Set up your tripod, look through the viewfinder and focus the camera. Get ready to release the shutter, then watch as a figure walks into the scene and leans upon a gate or a fence looking across at you.

2 There is something familiar about the other person. You recognize with astonishment that it is yourself. Immediately, you find that you are that figure, looking across at a photographer on the hillside, who is about to take a picture.

3 You realize that there is something familiar about the photographer: it is yourself. Immediately, you find yourself back once more on the hillside, preparing to take a picture of the scene opposite, which includes a figure nonchalantly leaning on a fence or a gate watching you.

4 Allow this switching between the photographer and the figure to take place several times. Finally, become the photographer, and watch as the figure opposite turns around, walks away and disappears from view. Take a picture of the empty scene, and feel your consciousness firmly located back within yourself.

The Art of Interpretation

" When read correctly, [dream] images tell us who we are instead of
who we think we are. They speak to us about our actual impact on
others, not about what we would like that impact to be. "
Montague Ullman

Dreams are a conversation between the unconscious and the conscious levels of the mind – levels that speak subtly different languages. Although the conscious mind may think that it understands what the unconscious is saying in dreams, it can, like a naive and inexperienced translator, make a nonsense of the true meaning. To grasp the real significance of our dreams, we must learn how to interpret them – a task that is in many ways more of an art than a science.

Although the language of dreams is in some respects consistent for us all, we have personal idiosyncrasies that render dream dictionaries, which ascribe specific or common meanings to dream experiences, of limited value. Dreams that arise from the personal unconscious (Level 2 dreams) are especially inclined to use images and associations from the dreamer's own life history and subjective inner world.

Successful dream interpretation depends on learning a few simple techniques and making a special study of your own dreams to unravel their very personal messages. Other people can make suggestions as to the meaning of your dreams, but only you can experience your inner world, and you are the final authority in interpreting the information that your unconscious is seeking to convey.

Reading Dream Language

Dreams speak a symbolic, visual language in which things are rarely what they seem. The two great schools of psychiatry offer different explanations for this. Sigmund Freud (1856–1939), the founder of psychoanalysis, believed that dreams use elaborate symbolic systems in order to protect us. The underlying meaning of a dream, he suggested, is often so disturbing that it would wake us from our slumbers and worry us deeply if it were presented undisguised. According to Carl Jung (1875–1961), however, symbols are the primal language of the unconscious, a pre-linguistic means of communication which presents truths potentially so mystical and profound that they can be understood only in terms of metaphor and allegory.

The strangeness and apparent illogicality of dream images are easier to penetrate if we seek to understand how the dreaming mind works.

Dream interpretation is best approached with an open mind. Play freely with the dream symbols that come to you, putting your mind into a relaxed, receptive state. There are two main techniques for interpreting dreams. Freud used *free association*, which involves allowing each aspect of a dream to stimulate a stream of unhindered associations. These eventually lead to a sudden insight that the dreamer recognizes as the essential hidden meaning.

Jung considered that free association takes the dreamer too far from the dream itself, and often misses its specific significance. His method of *direct association* was slightly different: instead of allowing the mind to freewheel, the dreamer returns to the dream image after each association.

The best way to illustrate the difference between free association and direct association is to take an image from a hypothetical dream and subject it to both methods. Suppose that you dreamed of a flight of stairs. In free association, you allow the image directly to inspire only the *first* association, speaking your thoughts aloud and leaving each subsequent image to be triggered by the one before in a "stream of consciousness". This method might produce the following:

" *stairs — ascent — climbing — high — fall — drowning — air — gasping — relief — dryness — wilderness — seeking — finding — surprise — mystery — gold locket* "

The gold locket suddenly brings to mind a Christmas long ago, when your mother received a gift of a beautiful gold locket from your father; you see again her eyes shining with joy, and a great wave of sadness comes over you as the dream reveals your deep longing for the warmth and security of the past.

In direct association, by contrast, you would write the word "stairs" in the middle of a sheet of paper, and proceed by writing your associations in a circle around it. Make sure you return to the word in the centre of the page after each association. This time, the result might be:

This method has resulted in a very different set of conclusions, which may indicate that the dream is revealing a deep insecurity, perhaps to do with professional life.

Dream Symbols

Objects that represent something other than themselves are either signs or symbols. Signs (for example, stop lights and corporate logos) are inventions of the conscious mind, with an artificial, limited and often local significance, which is always precise. Symbols, by contrast, present meaning through metaphor, sometimes obliquely, and are often resonant rather than exact in their connotations. The most powerful symbols are believed by Jungians to spring from the collective unconscious, appearing spontaneously across cultures and centuries, and carrying the same meaning everywhere: the cross, for example, is a universal symbol of the union of god with humankind.

Dreams, especially those from Levels 2 and 3, use symbols rather than signs to convey their messages from the unconscious. However, even the most powerful universal symbols can be reduced to the level of signs as a result of being consistently associated – at personal or cultural levels – with alien meanings. For example, the swastika, a sacred symbol for Buddhists, Hindus and Jains, is a sign of Nazi imperialism for most Westerners. If a swastika appears in a relatively superficial Level 1 dream, it might be directly related to Hitler's Third Reich; but in a Level 3 dream, a swastika might represent regeneration or harmony.

The first and most obvious associations suggested by a dream image may not, then, be the correct ones. It can take time and effort to uncover the deeper levels of meaning.

The bird, the leaf and the crescent are deeply symbolic images which resonate with multiple meanings – like all images from the natural world.

The Lance and the Wound

Case Study 3

The dreamer is a young postgraduate student, anxious to grow spiritually and to be of service to the world, but unsure what path to take.

" *I was standing naked on a hillside, and below me was the sea, blue and sunlit. The sun was warm on my body. Then I felt a pain, and saw a lance sticking in my side. A voice said, 'You too have a wound,' and I experienced intense happiness, as if I had received a blessing. I stretched out my arms and embraced the whole world in love and worship. I wondered if the lance in my side meant that I would become a healer, but the voice said, 'The world is healing.' I knew what this meant, but when I awoke the meaning escaped me. "*

In this dream the hill may symbolize achievement, the sea the creative unconscious, the sun divine energy, and nakedness purity. The lance and the wound, which might be interpreted by some as sexual symbols, are more likely to indicate that the dreamer is pierced by spiritual long-ings – for in dreams, even seemingly painful images may have a positive meaning. The dreamer embraces the world, and this symbolizes the far-reaching nature of spiritual realization. However, he is still only on the hillside, with some way still to climb. Egotistically, he mis-interprets the dream to mean that he may become a healer. The dream gently chides him for this: it is the world (the universal life-force) that heals, not the individual.

Dream Logic

Dream logic is as different from the logic of daily life as sleeping is from waking. Daily logic relies upon a set of well-charted laws that govern the way things behave. It is conveyed by language, which reflects an agreed and consistent relationship between phenomena and words. Dream logic, by contrast, expresses a world-view more like that of children who are too young to speak. It does not recognize a sharp division between inner and outer reality, and has no rigid "laws" into which we must strive to fit our personal experience.

The known, trusted logic of cause and effect is left behind in dreams, and replaced by a more intuitive and spontaneous system of meanings and connections.

Freud proposed that there is, in fact, a special kind of logic that runs through our dream life. He claimed that dreams express logical connections in four ways: *simultaneity* (objects and events presented together in the same dream), *contiguity* (objects and events occurring sequentially), *transformation* (one thing turning into another) and *similarity* (resemblances or associations between things). Of these, similarity, revealed primarily through indirect or direct association, is the most important, but one should look for all four of them when practising dream interpretation.

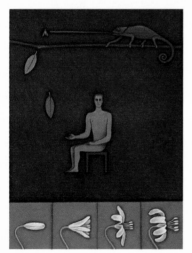

Another important consideration, identified by the American researchers Calvin Hall and Vernon Nordby, is *relative consistency* – that is, the frequency and uniformity with which dream motifs make their appearance. Ascertain the relative consistency in your own dream life by noting from your dream diary how often and in what guise the motifs occur. Then try to identify their meanings and the direct associations that they evoke.

The Procession

Case Study 4

A middle-aged businessman, mildly dissatisfied with his career, experienced this dream, one of a series which seemed to explore a contrast between his inner and outer lives.

" *I was in a passageway with many closed doors. I saw a man I knew years ago, dressed in black. I asked him for whom he was in mourning; he looked at me strangely, and said, 'Myself.' Then I was going down in an elevator so cramped that I couldn't stand upright. Suddenly I was in a huge hall with a high ceiling. Many couples were in a procession. I thought they were going up to an altar to be married, then I realized they were waiting for some kind of initiation ceremony. The couples at the front were people, but those further back were small furry animals, dressed and standing upright hand in hand. I had a sudden happy feeling.* "

The man from the past represents the idea of mourning, perhaps symbolizing the dreamer's regret for the past and his own lack of achievement. Contiguity follows — he feels that this lack of achievement traps him (the cramped elevator and the movement downward). Then comes transformation: the elevator becomes a vast hall, with couples joining together in a joyful ceremony. Association might reveal that the humans represent the dreamer's conscious, rational side, and the animals his natural, instinctive side; the message could be that the dreamer may still find inner harmony despite achieving little in professional life.

Dream Landscapes

Tantalizing, beautiful or awesome dream landscapes, perhaps seen only in fragments, are often the most lasting aspects of our dream life, haunting our memories long after the actual events of the dream are forgotten. The compelling, evocative quality of these visions suggests that they are not merely backgrounds to dream events, but an integral part of the messages that our dreams are seeking to convey.

Mountains usually indicate lofty aspirations. The dreamer is aware of exalted states of being that he or she longs to experience, but that remain out of reach. Paths up a mountain, or dreams of reaching the summit, can reassure the dreamer that important progress is being made.

The forest can represent the collective unconscious (see page 27). It is saturated in ambiguities — both a place of sanctuary and home to unpredictable primal energies and dark forces.

Rivers and valleys, sometimes interpreted as female sexual symbols, can be more general symbols of fertility, peace and safety.

**The
sea** *often
represents the deep
waters of the uncon-
scious;* **storms** *may symbolize
strong desire, passion or anger.*

Towns and cities
*can have a variety of
meanings, depending on how they
make the dreamer feel. Dreams of being lost in a
crowded city often represent the hectic confusion
of modern living.*

Crossroads
*are often a point of
decision. They might
symbolize either a coming
together or a parting of the ways.*

Temples, *with their inner sanctums, stand for private retreats
where the dreamer seeks peace. Any building set in a gloomy
landscape can signify the unconscious, and its doors can be the
gateways to the uncharted depths of the
dreamer's being.*

85

Dream Characters

Dream Cue

If you read a book before sleep, think about the character with whom you identify. Tell yourself that if this character appears in a dream, he or she will understand its meaning. If the figure does appear, try in the morning to see the dream from his or her point of view: you may find that this yields unexpected insights.

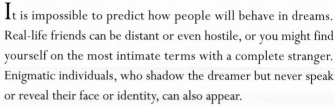

It is impossible to predict how people will behave in dreams. Real-life friends can be distant or even hostile, or you might find yourself on the most intimate terms with a complete stranger. Enigmatic individuals, who shadow the dreamer but never speak or reveal their face or identity, can also appear.

Before interpreting the role of the people you meet in dreams, search your dream diary for patterns. Do you dream more often of one sex than the other, of children or old people, of people you know or don't know? Are these dream characters helpful or unhelpful, friendly or frightening? How do you usually interact with them? How do they behave toward each other?

Scrutinize these patterns to try to see what overall message is being conveyed about your relationships. For example, ask yourself how you *see* the people in your dream life. Are they sharply defined, or vague and shadowy? If they are people you know, is their behaviour consistent with real life (suggesting that you feel secure with them), or do they reveal your hidden anxieties by failing to help you when you need them?

It helps to assess from which level of the mind the dream came. In Level 1 dreams, people often are exactly who they seem; but they might also represent aspects of yourself, as they often do at Level 2; while at Level 3 they might symbolize higher sources of wisdom. Dream characters can also represent generalized anxieties such as fear of old age or death, or behaviour or achievements to which the dreamer aspires. By giving human qualities to objects in dreams, the following exercise helps us to discover some of these hidden aspects of the self.

An Imaginary Dialogue

Dream Exercise 16

Try assigning an aspect of your own personality to the major motifs of your dream, using
the "empty chair" technique to enable these motifs to engage in a dialogue.

1 Examine a recent dream for significant
people, objects or events, and see what part
of yourself they might represent. For example, if you dreamed about a fast motorbike,
this might be the part of you that loves speed,
power and risk; if you dreamed about a cat,
this could be your lazy or cunning side.

2 Allow two of these motifs – the ones that
seem most significant – to talk. Place two
chairs opposite each other. Sit in one of them
and take the role of one dream aspect, speaking to the other aspect in the empty chair.
Move there to answer, then return to the first
chair to respond, and so on. Such a dialogue
might start with a wood accusing a road:

*The people in the cars you bring never stop to picnic
under my beautiful trees. They just rush through.*

The road replies: *That's because you're boring. They
all want to get to the big city on the other side.*

Wood: *That's not true. Everyone loves trees, and everyone needs a little peace and quiet.*

Road: *Most people wouldn't even know you were here
if it wasn't for me.*

A dialogue such as this might reveal two conflict-
ing sides of yourself: one longs for peace and natural beauty, while the other loves freedom and
the benefits of progress.

Introducing Archetypes

We all share powerful psychological energies relating to such aspects of body and mind as fertility, birth, death, sacrifice, love, transformation, resurrection, and courage. These primordial energies, which motivate, guide and inform the human race, are known as archetypes. They originate deep in the collective unconscious, the inherited set of impulses and memories shared by all of humankind, according to Jung.

Since archetypes are abstract energies, we cannot see them directly. Instead, they rise into awareness in dreams, personified symbolically as gods, heroes and other characters who feature in the mythology of all peoples and cultures. There are also archetypal narratives: the epic triumph over formidable challenges (for example, the labours of Hercules); or the pursuit of enlightenment (the quest for treasure, or the Holy Grail).

Mythical animals, such as dragons and unicorns, can be archetypal symbols of creative energy.

Archetypal energies can also appear in non-human form: for example, the four elements (earth, water, fire and air) represent the natural forces that shape and sustain our lives. Mythical creatures of the deep, such as sirens or mermaids, can be symbols of the collective unconscious itself. Even animals with particular qualities, such as the dog (loyalty) and falcon (clear-sightedness), can be archetypal symbols, some of which are exemplified by the animal-headed gods of ancient Egypt.

Carl Jung used the archetypal theme of descent into the underworld, symbolizing movement deep into the unconscious, to explore his own psyche. The exercise opposite is based on his method.

Digging into the Unconscious

Dream Exercise 17

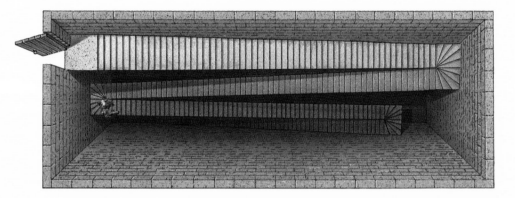

Jung compared intensive exploration of the unconscious to digging deep into the earth, discovering caves and underground galleries. We can use this imagery to stimulate dreams with archetypal content.

1 Before sleep, mentally prepare yourself to move downward into the earth, symbolizing movement down into your unconscious. Imagine yourself properly dressed for the descent, and equipped with any tools you need – perhaps a spade, ropes, or a flashlight.

2 Allow your imagination to provide all the details of your journey. Perhaps you will find a flight of stone steps winding down into the darkness. Or you might find yourself descending a mine shaft, entering a hollow tree trunk and climbing down into underground cabins formed by big roots, or even riding the setting sun into the underworld.

3 Let your unconscious bring you dream images or visions from the underground depths. Be prepared for the paradoxical transformation of movement downward into movement upward, as when underground caverns suddenly open out into an ethereal landscape. Going deeper into the unconscious, we may find ourselves coming into contact with our higher self – our innate spiritual wisdom and understanding.

4 In the morning, check your dreams carefully for the appearance of archetypes. There is no set pattern for this: dream experiences depend on the dreamer's circumstances.

Archetypal Characters

Dreamers sometimes wonder how to decide whether dream characters are archetypal or not. For example, if we dream of a woman with babies or of an old man, do these people represent themselves or the archetypal figures of Mother and Wise Old Man? There is a sense in which any dream character filling these roles would be archetypal, because motherhood itself and maturity itself are archetypal qualities. When true archetypes appear, however, they have an unforgettable impact on the dreamer.

The dreams in which true archetypes appear are recognized largely through their numinous quality – that is, their ability to inspire a sense of spiritual awe. Dreamers sometimes become convinced that the dreams were sent not by their own unconscious, but by a wise, beneficent force outside themselves.

An archetype may be present if you feel that the figure you have dreamed about is more important for some strong underlying theme than as a character in his or her own right. The universal relevance of archetypes can usually be felt as an experience of heightened significance – difficult to describe but hard to mistake once you have encountered it.

Jung saw archetypal dreams as having the special function of helping the dreamer to shape his or her future. He advised dreamers to ask why they had the dream, and to assess its potential impact. If archetypes are personifications of our psychic energies, then their appearance in dreams may be a pointer to our future path.

Lightning, symbol of the life force and of the divine spirit, is one of the dramatic natural phenomena that can herald the appearance of archetypes in dreams.

A Directory of Archetypes

As we have seen, archetypal energies can take many different forms, appearing in dreams as symbolic events or realistic or mythical beings. Initially, at least, the archetypes that appear in human form are most easily recognized.

The Anima

The Anima conveys wisdom, but of a kind directed inward rather than outward. Usually appearing in the form of a young woman, she represents the intuitive, feminine awareness in us all that men all too often neglect. The Anima, like the Animus, often acts as a guide for the dreamer, showing him or her not to be afraid to try new ways to explore the inner self.

The Animus

The Animus represents the masculine within the feminine. Often symbolized in dreams as a handsome young man, and appearing in fairy stories as a charming prince, this is the courageous, active, assertive masculine energy which women often allow to remain undeveloped in themselves. The Animus often appears in order to remind women to cease searching outside for qualities that are already present within themselves, and acts as a guide to show where these qualities can be found.

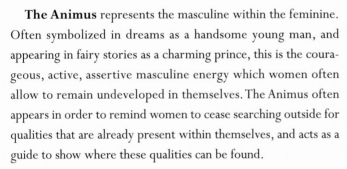

The Divine Child

The Divine Child, who appears in dreams as a baby or infant, is the archetype of regeneration and new life. The Divine Child is a combination of great innocence, purity and inviolability. It has the power to transform us by showing us our true origins as innocent, open-minded children, reminding us of what we have left behind and how far we have fallen short of our own early potential.

The Wise Old Man

The Wise Old Man brings knowledge and understanding to practical problems and dilemmas on our path of self-discovery and fulfilment. He might appear as magician, hermit, sage or teacher. Representing in part the accumulated wisdom of humanity, and in part the higher knowledge to which we aspire, he typically leaves the dreamer with a sense of personal strength and the power to make wise choices. This archetype may also appear in the form of a wise old woman.

The Hero

The Hero is the awakened inner self in both men and women that aspires to inner growth and development, and sets out on a quest for true understanding. The tasks facing the Hero are often symbolized as physical challenges requiring great skill and courage, and often necessitating the help of the Animus (from whom he is at times scarcely distinguishable), the Anima or the Wise Old Man. This archetype may also appear as an anti-hero – whose mistaken ideals lead him to enter a series of futile adventures from which he emerges with credit, but to no great effect. Whenever a dream involves physical or psychological challenges – fighting adversaries, climbing up or down a perilous slope, solving a difficult riddle – you can suspect that the Hero archetype is involved.

The Trickster

The Trickster has a light aspect, which can appear in dreams as a jester or clown, and a dark side, which presents itself as a sly, sinister figure whose pleasure is to meddle and wreck things. He or she switches easily between the two, usually without warning, and so can be a symbol of transformation. The Trickster represents our intuitive side, and although it may not feel like it at the time, his or her appearance and interference in our dreams is often to our long-term benefit.

The Mother, symbolizing fertility and the nurturing, loving care that makes growth possible, also has a darker side – that of the possessive, even devouring female, usually portrayed in fairy tales as a witch or a wicked stepmother. Worshipped as the bringer of harvests and as the all-powerful queen, the Mother is above all the essence of feminine bounty and mystery.

The Mother

The Shadow is the dark, repressed side of ourselves that can appear in dreams as a hostile companion or a silent, unsettling presence. The Shadow is not necessarily evil, but represents those parts of ourselves that we would rather keep hidden. We may need to bring the attributes represented by the Shadow into the open, where they can be consciously assessed and dealt with.

The Shadow

Numbers also carry archetypal significance in many of the great traditions. The number *one* represents the primary appearance of spirit in matter; the number *two*, male and female, and procreation; *three*, the heavenly trinity (and sometimes the trinity of body, mind and spirit); *four*, the earth and harmony; *five*, the human self (the five-pointed star); *six* (2 multiplied by 3), love, dreams and giving; *seven* (4 plus 3), the mystic journey which leads from earth to heaven; *eight*, initiation; *nine* (3 times 3), eternity and indestructibility; and *ten*, the law and the commandments (derived from our ten fingers). *Zero,* the perfect circle, simultaneously represents both infinity and the void: everything and nothing at all. Numbers may occur symbolically in dreams as a group of objects, companions, tasks and so on. Some traditions suggest that by carrying out specific rituals a set number of times before sleep we can induce dream material symbolized by the number concerned.

Working with Archetypes

The eight archetypal figures outlined in the previous four pages, based on Jung's major classification, are just a few of the countless ways in which our archetypal energies show themselves in dreams. By also accepting the elements (earth, water, air, fire) and such myth-laden creatures as unicorns and winged horses as archetypes, we gain for ourselves a rich psychic language with which to comprehend and interrogate our dreams.

Archetypes are valuable aids to dream interpretation, for they come with a ready-made cargo of easily-identifiable associations. We should be careful, however, not to fall into the trap of thinking that they provide instant meanings wherever they can be identified. Nor should we forget that they can only represent *parts* of the whole picture. Like all the components of the collective unconscious, such as myths and folktales, they are complex and often ambivalent: at the level of ultimate truths, there are no easy answers, only multi-faceted profundities.

Reading and contemplating the great stories of myth and literature makes it easier for us to identify archetypal events, patterns and characters in our dreams.

If we familiarize ourselves with the archetypes, and with their appearance in myths, we will become aware of them when they appear in our dreams, and will be more open to their messages; being familiar with them may even make them more likely to manifest themselves. As archetypes spring from the deepest levels of our own unconscious, dreams that bring us into closer contact with them also bring us into a more harmonious relationship with our own self. At the same time, we gain a set of models (or agents, acting on our behalf) which can help us explore the meanings of a Level 2 or Level 3 dream – in the same way that Tarot cards can help us to arrive at a fuller understanding of our innermost character.

Identifying Your Personal Archetypes

Dream Exercise 18

Archetypes carry universal meaning, but we all add details from our personal waking and dreaming experiences. When interpreting archetypal dreams, it is important to be aware of any personal significance that particular archetypes may have for you.

1 Select those archetypes that seem to carry the most emotional charge for you, trying if possible to choose not only archetypal characters but also archetypal objects, activities or numbers.

2 Write the name of each of these important archetypes in the centre of a separate page of your dream diary, and surround each one with the associations and dream memories they bring to mind.

3 At the bottom of each page, write down brief notes on the dreams in which the

archetype appeared. In this way, build up a picture of what the archetype means to you personally, and of the context and the frequency in which he, she or it makes dream appearances.

4 You may discover that your own concepts of the archetypes are incongruous at some points with those of the great myths (see pages 96–8). Ask yourself why. Are you, for example, resisting through inhibition or obstinacy the path indicated by the myth? If so, think what you can do to change yourself and to overcome the obstacle.

Amplification

Once archetypes have been identified in dreams, preliminary interpretation is often straightforward, as their universal symbolic meanings have been thoroughly explored. However, these meanings tend to be overlaid by more subjective associations, so that the deeper levels of meaning belonging to each archetype, together with its specific relevance to the dreamer, will emerge only after more detailed work.

The story of Shiva, the father of the "holy family" in the Hindu pantheon, offers a wide range of archetypal events and imagery, lending itself well to amplification.

Jung believed that such work should take the form of amplification – exploring the myths in which the archetype concerned appears, and becoming aware of how these myths reflect aspects of your own life. Read the myths, and ponder on them in your waking hours. For Westerners, Jung considered the Greek myths especially suitable, but you may prefer mythology from other cultures: you could choose native American, Egyptian or Hindu myths, shamanic stories or Celtic tales.

Imagine that you have dreamed about a young man with a broken guitar. Through amplification you might associate this figure with Orpheus, the Greek musician whose songs charmed even the animals, and this in turn might conjure up the story of how Orpheus entered the land of the dead in order to rescue his love Eurydice. In looking back toward Eurydice as he walked ahead of her into the light, Orpheus disobeyed a crucial taboo, and lost his love forever. This episode might suggest guilt or the feeling of losing a prize through

one's own carelessness. By exploring the myth further
with this in mind, or by tracing other aspects of the
narrative, you may start to see aspects of your own life
in a new light, and build on such perceptions to reach an
improved state of self-knowledge.

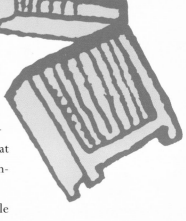

The more you familiarize yourself with the great myths,
the easier amplification becomes. Some myths will seem intuitively appropriate to your circumstances, but all the great
mythological themes have emerged from the collective unconscious, and all have important links with the human psyche.

In the course of amplification you may wish to take the role
of the archetype yourself, imagining that you are inside the
myth, participating in the events in order to ascertain the
myth's immediate personal relevance. Alternatively, you may
watch from the sidelines as one of the minor characters, or
become an objective observer of the action.

During amplification, you may also feel the need to change
parts of the myth. It is perfectly legitimate to do so, by altering
or adding details, so long as the main themes are kept intact,
and the archetypal strength of the story remains uncompromised. You may also find that once you begin working with the
myth, it makes a direct appearance in your dreams, providing
further clarification and guidance.

If you fail to have – or to remember – archetypal dreams,
choose a myth that appears to parallel your circumstances.
Make a point of meditating on the myth and pondering it, writing about and drawing it, requesting all the time that your
unconscious introduces it into your dreams.

Amplification can even be practised when you cannot identify a particular myth that relates to your personal situation.
Instead, choose a myth that has relevance for us all, such as the
story of Persephone, daughter of Demeter, goddess of agricul-

Dream Cue

---

*Build up your own
mythic repertoire to
use in amplification.
The Greek myths of
Jason and the Golden
Fleece, and the tale
of Oedipus, provide
good starting points.
The tale of Pandora's
Box, with its expla-
nation of how human
ills came into the
world, is another
one: when Pandora,
out of curiosity,
opened the container
she had been given,
sickness, toil and
conflict flew out into
the world, leaving
only hope remaining
inside.*

ture and fertility. Persephone was abducted by Hades, lord of the underworld, and carried off to his kingdom. On hearing the news, Demeter went into mourning, bringing winter to the world. Zeus later persuaded Hades to set Persephone free for part of the year, but she had to remain in the underworld for the remaining two-thirds. The grand themes in this myth (youth/age, winter/summer, earth/hell, freedom/captivity) make it an especially resonant subject for amplification.

The dreaming mind often represents the underworld as a cave, basement, or dark night, and in doing so may be emphasizing that most of us are fated from time to time to visit the symbolic underworld of grief or despair. But the Persephone myth goes on to show us that the underworld is ultimately not about death and oblivion, but about incubation and rebirth. When Persephone reappears in the upper world, she brings the spring, and life makes a triumphant return to the land.

Another universal Greek myth is that of Hercules, ordered by Zeus to serve a master who gave him twelve apparently impossible labours to perform. He overcame every difficulty, and was rewarded by being made immortal. Look for the appearance of difficult symbolic tasks in your dreams, and notice not only how you tackle them but your state of mind in doing so. If the tasks seem completely beyond you, instruct yourself on waking that you will be more determined next time, and look out for signs of greater success in your dreams.

Finding the right myth for amplification is sometimes simply a matter of trial and error. While you are searching for the appropriate narrative, be prepared to try a number of stories before you find one that fits well.

Shedding the Ego's Trappings

Case Study 5

This dreamer is a young dancer, and it is appropriate that in her amplification she uses the legend of Ishtar – the goddess who performed the original Dance of the Seven Veils.

" *In my dream I was in a dark tunnel going downward, searching for something important. At the first bend a man at a turnstile demanded money to let me pass. Further on the same thing happened at an iron gate, barred like a prison. I had no cash, so I took a silver ring from my finger. Then the tunnel opened into a space like a floodlit parking lot. There were people watching from banks of seats, and they shouted that I had to sing before I could pass. Thankfully the dream ended there.* "

" *When I tried amplification, I thought of the Egyptian Book of the Dead, where the soul has to give something to pass each guardian. Then I thought of the ancient Greeks paying the boatman to ferry them across the Styx. But neither of these themes felt quite right to me.* "

" *Later, I suddenly thought of the Babylonian myth of Ishtar, who has to leave her jewels and finery at each of the seven gates of the underworld, and arrive naked to meet her dark sister Ereshkigal, who reigns there as queen. This made immediate sense. The dream was saying that I must lose layers of my tough ego if I want to penetrate my unconscious and meet my hidden self. It's given me a lot to think about.* "

Personal Mythology

The word "myth" is often used as a synonym for fiction, and certainly the events in myths happened so long ago that there is no way of knowing whether they bear any relation to historical events. Research, however, often suggests that they contain elements of fact. For example, many researchers believe that the legendary hero Hercules is based on a real Greek chieftain; and Troy, for centuries dismissed as a fictional city, has since been excavated by archaeologists.

Legendary events may have their roots in history. The great floods of the Bible and other epics are probably based on actual inundations, long in the past. However, this in no way limits their profound archetypal significance.

Whatever relationship myths have with facts, they are all true in one sense: they represent situations that occur over and over again, not only in the outer world but in our inner lives as well. They warn us of the pitfalls of certain courses of action, opening up new areas of self-understanding and giving us insights into spiritual realities that cannot be expressed in anything other than metaphorical terms.

We can apply our own creative instincts to encourage the imagination to work with the unconscious. One way to do this, and to assimilate the dreams that do not seem to correlate with any existing archetypes, is to create your own personal myth. You could draw this as a series of pictures or a cartoon strip; if you are musical, you could even compose an appropriate ballad. Most people, however, will probably be content to write down the episodes of the myth in their dream diary. Like the great myths of the past, your story will "grow" organically with time.

Writing Your Own Myth

Dream Exercise 19

After you have been keeping a dream diary for some weeks, you may find that you can recognize recurrent themes or characters that have an archetypal feel, even though no archetypal aspects can be readily identified. These are part of a myth unique to you.

1 Search your dream diary for dreams that seem to hold particular personal significance to you. They may appear to be linked, revealing a theme that runs through your dream life. Tease out the possible archetypal meaning of these dreams by looking upon them as episodes in a myth specific to yourself.

2 Weave these episodes together into a story, allowing your imagination to provide background and colour. Give your dream characters the power to interact freely, and observe the result carefully. If there are gaps in the narrative, instruct your unconscious to fill them for you in future dreams.

3 Record the story, and the emotions it arouses, in your dream diary, and try illustrating them in your dream sketch book. Give the characters in your personal myths names, either mythical or invented. Pay attention to the emotions that arise as you tell this story.

4 This personal myth represents a situation or preoccupation that you have not yet fully worked through in waking life. Through narrative and characterization, it voices your innermost concerns to your conscious mind. The myth may stretch back across many years, reflecting your path through life, and will probably hold clues about the future.

Wish-fulfilment

Freud's clinical experience led him to believe that dreams have a strong element of wish-fulfilment, acting out the instincts and desires that we are unable to satisfy in waking life. Subsequent dream theories also acknowledge the importance of wish-fulfilment, although they lay less emphasis on this than Freud did.

Wish-fulfilment dreams often have sexual, violent or acquisitive themes. When analyzing them, the dreamer may be ashamed of these dream actions, and see them as wholly unrepresentative of his or her true nature. The deeds may be carried out not by the dreamer in person but by someone else representing an aspect of the dreamer's personality, a device that often prevents the conscious mind from recognizing the dream's real purpose.

Although these dreams can give us unsettling insights into our hidden desires, they need not necessarily be viewed in a negative light. Many of the desires so revealed are perfectly innocent, but were denied expression during childhood. Children's self-assertion, individuality, sexuality and even creativity are often discouraged by disapproving adults, and wish-fulfilment dreams perform a very useful function in bringing such repression to our attention. We can then start to explore the reasons behind any feelings of defeat and frustration in life, and to try to find ways of overcoming our problems.

The following dream, an adapted version of a remarkable case in Freud's *Interpretation of Dreams,* eloquently demonstrates how symbols can conceal the meaning of a vivid wish-fulfilment dream.

Animals in dreams can act out desires that the dreamer feels unable to express in real life.

A Cry for Love

Case Study 6

This graphic example of a dream of sexual
wish-fulfilment was told to Freud by a policeman's wife.

*" I dreamed that there was a break-in at my house, and I called out in fear for
a policeman. But the policeman was in church at the time, accompanied by two
tramps. There were steps in front of the church, and a path leading to a hill
and to thick woods behind. The policeman was bearded, and wearing his
helmet, brass collar and cloak, while the tramps had sack-like aprons
around their middles. "*

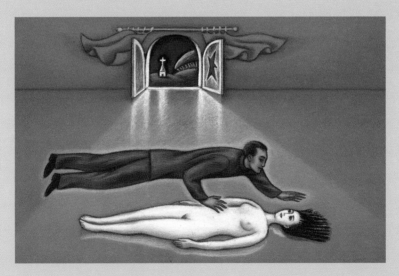

Freud believed that there were a number of sexual symbols in the dream. The church
represents the vagina, the steps sexual intercourse, the hill and the woods are the female pubic
mound and hair, the policeman's cloak is a phallic symbol, and the sack-like aprons are the
scrotum. On the strength of these symbols, Freud suggested that the woman wants more
sexual contact with her husband. Someone "breaks into" her house (a disturbing sexual urge
"breaks into" her awareness), and although she mistakes her arousal for fear, her dream
symbolically — and, it has to be said, with some ingenuity — spells out her desire.

A Dreamer's
Guide to the Whole Self

*" The experience of dreaming ... affords a growth-enhancing
encounter with other aspects of ourselves. "*
Montague Ullman and Nan Zimmerman

We all have three aspects: mind, body and spirit. When they work together harmoniously, we achieve wholeness: sometimes, however, they are in conflict, and need to be integrated. Dreams, our windows into the unconscious, can help to provide the missing threads that bind together our intellectual, physical and spiritual sides.

Doctors now recognize that conflicts between mind and body play a large role in physical illness. But the effects of conflict between mind and *spirit* – the aspect of ourselves that represents our sense of identity, and expresses itself through religion and the creative arts – are less well-known. The spirit is home to our sense of wonder, and is capable of feeling awe not just at the outer world, but at the mysteries of its own being. Scientific explanations of life in purely material terms can beguile our minds and make us deaf to the promptings of the spirit, leaving us without any real sense of meaning or purpose.

Dreams can show us a way back to our true sense of identity by bringing out the buried parts of our unconscious. By giving us glimpses of our inner lives, dreams have the power to reveal our unconscious motives and provide vital insights into the fundamental truths we have left behind. If we heed the

lessons of our dreams, we will no longer be dominated by the mundane events of the day. We will regain the wholeness that is our birthright.

Toward the Whole Self

Many cultures have seen dreams as a path toward healing and wisdom. The ancient Greeks and Egyptians thought that dreams could reveal the cause and cure of mental and physical problems. In Siberia, the Americas and Africa, shamans are widely held to obtain guidance for people with various afflictions by visiting other worlds in their dreams. In Arab, ancient Chinese, Hindu and Buddhist traditions, dreams are seen as providing insights and warnings relevant to both the inner and the outer life. In much the same way, modern psychologists regard dreams as revealing the causes of neurosis. Jung, in particular, said that dreams can chart and further the healing process for mind, body and spirit.

Inner conflicts sometimes lay the foundations of deep psychological difficulties. By resolving these unconscious conflicts, we can move toward wholeness and peace.

Many of the more recent self-help movements use dreams to uncover buried personal metaphors which can then be used not just in healing, but also in guiding personal development. The self-discoveries revealed in dreams are harnessed in psychosyn-

thesis, a combination of treatments designed to help the integration of various aspects of the self. Dreams also provide some of the raw material for creative arts therapies, which use music, drama and painting to help people to express hitherto suppressed or unarticulated aspects of themselves.

Dreams offer different keys to unlock the doors to self-integration and the reconciling of mind, body and spirit. They provide a "way in" to the spirit itself, enabling us to understand its needs and concerns more completely. By allow-

ing the innermost self to express itself freely, dreams create an important bridge between our inner and outer lives, affording a unique chance to listen to and learn from our inner wisdom.

As you move toward the greater self-understanding that marks integration, your dreams will help you to monitor your progress. Look for an increase in Level 2 and Level 3 dreams, together with a feeling that you are being given access to "universal" or "eternal" truths. Certain themes are also valuable indicators of progress toward the whole self: dreams of meeting old and wise characters, searching and finding, travelling (especially crossing rivers or boundaries) and exquisite scenery all tend to make more frequent appearances.

Dreams sometimes symbolize integration of body, mind and spirit by strains of music or snatches of poetry. Lucid dreams also increase in number, as does the ability to influence the content of dreams. In this way, an enriched dream life both nourishes and reflects an enriched wholeness of the self.

__Getting in touch__ with the aspects of yourself from which you have become distanced, gathering them in from exile and bringing them into harmony with each other, are key tasks in the quest for the whole self.

Self-understanding

Before we embark on a journey, we usually plan our route, tracing all the steps to our destination. The first step on the road toward inner wholeness is to locate our starting point, and to understand where — and who — we are now. Dreams, with their power to reveal our innermost hopes and fears, are invaluable allies in the attempt to reach this self-understanding.

Dreams show us what we are really like, offering a true reflection of ourselves which reveals our hidden depths as well as our weaknesses.

Many of the processes involved in personal integration take place below the level of consciousness. Once the unconscious recognizes our aims, it sets about helping us to realize them — in much the same way as it helps to solve practical or intellectual problems. However, much of the work of understanding the self must be done at the conscious level. We must consciously recognize the tensions caused when the body is put under strain by the mind, or when the mind is ignoring the promptings of the spirit, and consciously decide to make the necessary adjustments to our attitudes and lives.

The different levels of dreaming assist this process in different ways. Level 1 dreams, which may appear to portray trivial events, help us to acknowledge many of the upsets of daily life. In the search for self-understanding, we have to ask why these experiences were important enough to be relived in dreams. By studying them, we can begin to identify aspects of our lives that may need attention. For example, our dreams may be telling us about neglected physical problems, or reminding us of an interest that we have allowed to lapse, or revealing undesirable tendencies such as avoiding responsibility, over-work or over-reacting to mild irritations. In short, they tell us, in the simplest terms, *what* is wrong.

The deeper dreams found at Level 2, on the other hand, show us *why* we are the way we are. By revealing the experiences that have helped to develop and shape our personalities – the building blocks of our lives – Level 2 dreams help us to recognize the energies and repressions of our inner lives, and to see the unconscious motives underlying much of our behaviour. They portray the workings of what Freud called the *id*, the instinctive side of ourselves which is controlled during our waking hours by the ego.

Dreams from Level 3 – the deepest level of the mind – provide insights from the accumulated wisdom of the collective unconscious. The archetypal characters and events that they contain are capable of revealing *who* we are. We should also look out for glimpses of Level 3 material in the more common Level 2 dreams – perhaps encountering a mysterious young woman who shows us the way safely through a dark wood, meeting a wise old man who offers us words of wisdom, seeing an extraordinary landscape or hearing vivid, heavenly music.

We can help self-understanding not only by studying our dreams carefully, but by asking ourselves the right questions, keeping them in the forefront of awareness as much as possible during the day and before retiring to sleep. The fundamental question is, of course, "Who am I?", but you may prefer to ask, "Why am I here?" or "What is this all about?" An answer, or partial answer, may appear symbolically in dreams, or take the form of a new inner conviction, as if you have absorbed the meaning of a reply that cannot itself be held in the memory.

Dream Cue

Scan your dreams for any signs of uncertainty about your direction through life. Ask yourself whether your dreams reveal fear of the unknown, or doubt as to whether to continue on the road ahead. Before sleep, meditate on the path your life has taken, and ask your dreams to show you the way forward.

Revealing the True Self

Dream Exercise 20

In our waking lives we play many different parts, which can appear in exaggerated form in our dreams. This exercise will help us to analyze these exaggerations and to detect the clues they hold to the "real me".

1 Look through your dream diary and list the roles that you have played in your dreams. Perhaps you have been a car- or train-driver, a lover, a parent, or a business executive; perhaps you have appeared as a traveller, a reporter, a child, a prisoner, an actor, or even a witch or a magician.

2 Draw a circle on a large sheet of paper. Around the outside, write down the names of your dream roles, or draw a sketch of them. Look at these roles and think about them carefully, bearing in mind that each of the characters on the circumference are different aspects of yourself.

3 Focus on the blank space in the centre of the circle, and ask yourself: who is the person in the centre? Without consciously trying to "think up" an answer, try to visualize an image or words appearing spontaneously inside the circle.

4 If nothing happens, scan the images or names around the circumference again, without pausing or dwelling on any associations they might prompt. Then look again at the blank space in the centre. Repeat the exercise patiently until your unconscious supplies a hint of some kind that seems to offer an insight into your essential identity.

Aspects of the Body

Dream Exercise 21

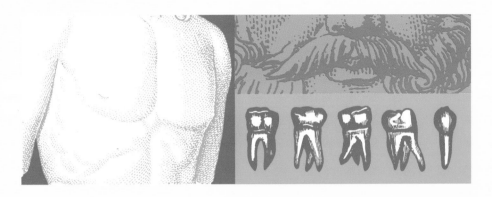

Our true feelings about ourselves are often symbolized in dreams by distortions in our body image. This exercise is designed to explore the nature of such alterations, and to discover what they reveal about our hidden inner conflicts.

1 Note down on a piece of paper all the aspects of your own physical appearance in dreams. You may dream of yourself as younger or older than you really are, or find yourself fatter or thinner, uglier or better-looking. Notice, also, whether you have any unusual characteristics, such as blemishes or exaggerated or shrunken features.

2 Ask yourself whether your dream image is compensating for some perceived physical inadequacy. If so, ask your dreaming mind to help you accept and value your appearance, and instruct it to show you as you really are in future.

3 Use association to try to find out whether your dream self-image symbolizes any mental or emotional characteristics. Skin blemishes might suggest negative inner feelings on show to the world; an elaborate hairstyle can indicate vanity; and teeth could represent verbal aggression.

4 If your dream image involves a drastic transformation of appearance and character, try to find the underlying meaning. A change of sex, for example, might imply that you need to develop the opposite side of your nature; becoming an animal may show a need to be more in touch with your instincts.

Self-communication

A string quartet or a theatre company can mount a perfectly adequate performance by playing well as individuals, but it is only by working closely *together*, trusting and helping each other, that they can produce true excellence. In much the same way, many people go through life "on autopilot", with their mind, body and spirit acting independently – collaborating, but not co-operating wholeheartedly in unison.

The common impression we have about ourselves that our heart goes one way and our head goes another, or that we are not really sure what we think or feel about something, is a strong indicator that the different parts of our inner selves are not communicating effectively; and so are the feelings of being generally dispirited, soulless or jaded. If we are to progress toward wholeness, we need to strengthen the links between our mind, body and spirit, opening up clearer channels for them to speak to each other. As we do so, we will come into ever closer contact with our instinctive energies.

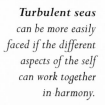

Turbulent seas can be more easily faced if the different aspects of the self can work together in harmony.

These energies – inherited impulses that propel us toward particular actions, fall into two categories: on the one hand, there are basic drives, such as sex, hunger and aversion from danger; and on the other, more complex motivations, such as love, the appreciation of beauty and our sense of morality. If we overrule these higher instincts (perhaps by opting to work late when we know that we should spend more time at home), our dreams may remind us of our true priorities – as in the case study opposite. Self-communication is

Panic in the Street

Case Study 7

The dreamer is a housewife and mother who has given up a career to raise her family – but feels that she has not yet regained full contact with her nurturing instincts.

" In my dream I was leading three dogs, which I was training to respond to a whistle. I let them off the leash, and to my horror they immediately ran away toward a busy road. They took no notice of my whistle, so I started to call them, but suddenly found that I had forgotten their names. I ran after them in panic, but lost them in the road. I asked some people if they had seen them, but they looked at me as if I were stupid. Then I saw one of the dogs across the road. It seemed to be laughing at me."

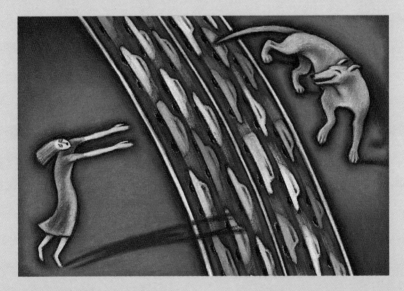

Animals in dreams sometimes represent our instinctive side. This dream may be indicating that the dreamer cannot understand or control her instinctive energies. When she tries to call the dogs, she has forgotten how to do so (she cannot remember their names). There is danger in her lack of control (the busy road), but she also finds difficulty in communicating her problems to others. One of the dogs has crossed the road (become even less accessible), and mocks her, suggesting that we can never be comfortable with ourselves if we lose contact with our instinctive life.

partly about tuning in to our instinctive energies and finding out how to allow our positive instincts to grow, while keeping any negative instincts under the control of the conscience.

The voice of instinct, however, is often drowned out by the babble of our daily concerns, or by the persistent background noise of longstanding worries that we have allowed to grow out of proportion. The exercise opposite is a good way to encourage our dreams to put such problems in their true perspective. Reflect, also, on any dreams in which the characters are revealed by interpretation to be different aspects of ourselves. Note how the characters behave toward each other, and use direct association (see page 78) to find out what internal frictions or blind spots these characters might represent.

The empty chair technique (see page 87), which enables aspects of your dream self to talk to each other, is another valuable aid to dealing with any negative instincts or persistent worries uncovered by interpretation. Ask for your dreams to continue the dialogue and to provide further clarification and possible solutions; once the problems are recognized, they must be worked with at the conscious level.

Different aspects of the self, freed to express themselves in dreams, engage in constant discussions, arguments and collusions.

Conducting healthy relationships with others, too, depends on our having a good relationship with ourselves. We may think that we are good at telling others our thoughts and feelings, but our unconscious sometimes knows better, and tells us so in symbolic dreams – of waiting for letters that never arrive, of inability to hear or to make oneself heard. If dreams reveal shortcomings in the ways in which we interact with others, true self-communication may only be possible if we work on our external communication skills as well.

Throwing the Switch

Dream Exercise 22

This exercise uses visualization to help to identify and to banish the inner problems
revealed by dream work. It is a way to activate our inner energy,
galvanizing all the aspects of the self into constructive action.

1 Close your eyes and imagine a house at night. You are standing outside, looking up at the darkened windows; walk forward, open the front door, and head toward the basement stairs.

2 Pause at the door at the top of the basement stairs, knowing that your current problems and difficulties lurk below. Conquer your feeling of unease, open the door and start walking down the dark stairs.

3 At the bottom of the stairs, grope along the wall until you find a large, heavy switch. Take a deep breath, then throw it.

4 At once, the basement is flooded with bright light. See how harmless are the problems that held such menace in the darkness. Look in turn at the images that represent them – perhaps broken objects to be mended, letters to be burned, childhood things to be put away.

5 Gather these objects together and climb back into the house. Each room is now a blaze of welcoming light, and it is easy to see how to put each problem to rights. Ask your dreams to give you the energy to set to work. Open your eyes and return to the present, feeling strong and optimistic.

Toward Calmer Dreams

We remember more bad dreams than good, and most of our bad dreams are at least mildly anxious. Worry, which is really a type of fear, is a useful aspect of our nature, for it keeps us on our guard for approaching danger. However, our anxieties can easily slip out of our control and become problems in their own right. This may be because we were never shown how to deal with them during our formative childhood years, or because of social conditioning. Common culprits are: guilt associated with our own emotional needs; the quest for social approval and worldly success; and greed for material possessions. In working life, of course, anxiety can easily be triggered by excessive professional demands or by job insecurity and other uncertainties.

We may be able to ignore or rationalize these anxieties in waking life, but not so in our dreams, which keep us in touch with our unconscious, drawing attention to our innermost fears and giving us an opportunity to acknowledge and deal with them. By careful interpretation and association, we can delve beyond the apparent reasons for our worried state of mind to discover the real, deep-seated cause of our difficulties.

Worries about social skills, for example, are revealed when a dreamer finds himself or herself ridiculed, shunned or inappropriately dressed at a gathering. Personal relationships supply another common theme: a dreamer may search vainly for a loved one in a vast city, or find him or her in the arms of someone else. Insecurity, or feeling overwhelmed by responsibilities or other people, can be symbolized in dreams involving falling, drowning, being buried alive or being crushed in a crowd. Such long-standing anxieties can become fixtures in our psychological life,

and dreams will draw them to our attention until we address them at the conscious level. We can then find out why we have these problems, and plan a course of action to put matters right.

When dealing with such dreams, start by establishing, primarily by direct association (see page 78), whether or not the symbolism relates to something you know about already in waking life. Anxieties arising from consciously acknowledged situations usually appear in relatively undisguised form: for example, you may dream of failing an examination, and recognize this as linked to a very real fear of being passed over for an important promotion. Forgotten or repressed traumas, on the other hand, are more likely to appear in symbolic form: a dream of being pinned down by mechanical, doll-like creatures, for example, may prove on close analysis to relate to a hitherto

Take control of your inner fears by confronting the insights supplied by dreams – your fears may never evaporate, but you should be able to shrink them to a truer perspective.

unacknowledged tendency to emotional repression; dreams of suffocation may relate to a feeling of being dominated; and dreams of being trapped at every turn might indicate that you find yourself placed unjustly in the wrong by others.

An especially common source of stress, and therefore of anxiety dreams, is loss of control over one's life. Vital decisions affecting career, health or relationships are taken out of your hands, leaving you feeling like a helpless bystander or a puppet manipulated by others. Dreams can both reflect this stress and urge the dreamer to deal with it constructively.

If your dreams relate to acknowledged anxieties, examine them carefully to see whether they suggest a way of coming to terms with your vulnerabilities. Try discussing the problems with other people, and preparing fully for the challenges that lie ahead. Anxieties that arise from unacknowledged fears, or from repressed past experiences, require much deeper levels of self-understanding: their essential lesson is that we must come to accept ourselves for what we are before we can start to bring about any changes.

Unfortunately, the dream that reveals an anxiety may not tell the dreamer what action he or she should take. However, the unconscious can be cajoled into supplying suggestions. Cease your attempts at conscious solutions, and go to sleep holding the dilemma in your mind. Relax, secure in the knowledge that the problem has now been handed over to a wise and trustworthy friend who will ponder it carefully. Keep a close eye on your dream diary, as the answers (or partial answers) may come hidden in an apparently unrelated dream, or in a symbolic form that needs interpreting. It may be several nights before a useful clue appears, but with patience there is every chance that it will. Remember to thank your unconscious afterward; like the conscious mind, it thrives on encouragement.

Dream Cue

Ask a friend to scan your dream diary, and to choose two recent nightmares or disturbing dreams. Decide which of the dreams you found the more upsetting, and attempt to explain to your friend why. As you weigh the two dreams against each other, encourage your collaborator to ask gently probing questions, which may lead to the un-covering of deep concerns that you have not previously acknowledged.

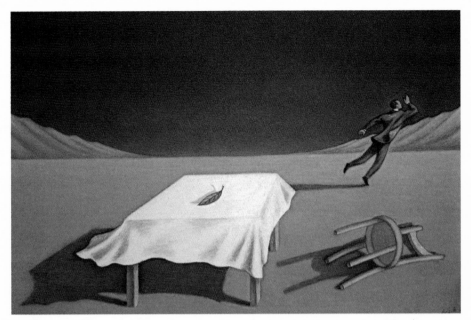

Sometimes our unease stems more from "free-floating anxiety" – general feelings of tension and doubt – than from specific problems. In such circumstances, dreams can help the unconscious to improve its self-image, which will in turn affect our conscious behaviour. Draw a picture that symbolizes your anxieties, and tell yourself that an artist will redraw it in the dream world so that it represents more closely the person you want to be. Watch for any improvement in your dream self-image, destroy your original picture and draw a new one that reflects this change. Include it in your dream sketch book, noting also any progress in your waking life.

The following case studies (pages 120–121) illustrate two anxiety dreams. The first relates to an everyday problem which can be dealt with by direct action; the second reflects a deep-seated insecurity which can only be resolved by further work with the unconscious.

Identifying
and isolating the anxieties that surface in our dreams are the essential preparations to freeing ourselves from them.

An Office Catastrophe

Case Study 8

The dreamer is a manager in a large financial institution, who is currently experiencing a period of high stress at work as a result of reorganization.

" I was sitting by my open office window when a strong wind blew, and papers started to fly off my desk and out of the window. I threw myself across the desk to try to save them, and then tried to close the window, but it was stuck. I flung myself through it to catch the sheets that had blown out. But instead of being on the ground floor as it really is, my office in the dream was high up, and I found myself clinging to a small ledge outside. Far below I could see my precious documents floating toward the ground. I called for help, but nobody came, and I found myself falling and falling. "

The dream reflects the dreamer's feelings of powerlessness at work. The papers on his desk are disrupted by capricious forces (the wind), about which he can do nothing (the window is stuck). In trying to assert himself (catch the papers), he risks his professional position, already insecure (his office is at the top of the building). He also feels that he lacks allies at work – no one is there to help him as he frantically clings on, and finally he loses everything. The dream helped the manager to recognize the strain that he was under, prompting him to take stock of his situation and to devote more time to dealing efficiently with the problems that most troubled him.

Betrayal in the Park

Case Study 9

The dreamer is a professional woman in her 40s, who has recently emerged emotionally shaken after the collapse of a long-standing relationship.

" *It was a warm, sunny day and I was walking to my favourite restaurant near my home. When I came to the restaurant, there was just a blank wall. I felt confused and turned away, but the familiar street had disappeared, and I was in a small deserted public park, under a grey sky. I felt a terrible dread, as if something awful was about to happen. I couldn't find a way out, but to my relief a park attendant appeared, walking ahead of me along one of the winding paths. I tried to catch up with him, but he kept just ahead. In despair I grabbed his arm, but he crumbled into dust, and we fell into a sort of open grave.* "

The dream shows several features of nightmares: being lost (familiar landmarks disappear), transformation (the sunshine replaced by a dark sky), being trapped (there is no exit from the park), and, worst of all, a refuge or friendly person (the park attendant) turning into a terror worse even than that from which the dreamer is fleeing. Interpretation revealed that the dreamer has deep insecurities that make it hard to trust others: a world that once seemed meaningful and predictable now seems alien and threatening to her. The dreamer now came to see how much depended on her ability to recover her faith and, ultimately, to command love.

How to Neutralize Nightmares

For all their unpleasantness, nightmares serve a useful function: they draw our attention to the fears and forebodings that hatch in our unconscious and have an impact on our waking life. Even if the actual content of a dream seems harmless, all dreams that convey a sense of menace, terror or loathing can be classed as nightmares. Typically, the dreamer feels threatened by something against which he or she has no defence, and which often remains cloaked in darkness.

Aggression is a common theme of nightmares. People fighting may reflect a conflict between aspects of the dreamer's conscious and unconscious minds.

The most frequently reported nightmare theme is of being chased, yet being unable to move. This might be because the dreamer becomes subliminally aware of the loss of muscle tone which accompanies dreaming, but a more likely explanation is that it represents the primal fear of being helpless in the face of danger, like a rabbit trapped in the headlights of a speeding car.

Paradoxically, some frightening dreams fail to arouse any strong emotion. Subsequent interpretation often reveals that this is because the alarming events symbolize something that carries no intrinsic terror. For example, a dream of shooting an assailant could symbolize the power to overcome obstacles.

If you are troubled by a particular recurring nightmare, you may wish to visualize a special helper when you are awake, who will be available to be summoned in the dream to help you banish or conquer your fears. The exercise opposite is designed to help you find such an ally.

Enlisting a Dream Helper

Dream Exercise 23

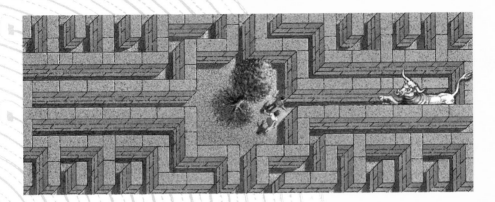

When themes or specific details repeat themselves in dreams, sometimes over many years, this suggests a powerful issue of some kind waiting to be resolved. A dream helper can assist you to identify this issue and to lay it to rest.

1 Create an image of a man, woman or animal that you would like to help you deal with your troubled dream life. He, she or it may be entirely imaginary, or based upon someone you know. Your helper might be a mythological character, a hero from the movies or from books, or a helpful person whom you have already met in dreams. Visualize your helper in as much detail as possible, and think of an appropriate name.

2 Imagine that you are back in the dream, and summon your dream helper. Enjoy the certainty that whatever frightens you will now be transformed into something without any power to harm you. Ask your helper to assist you in effecting this transformation – perhaps by chasing the demon away.

3 Impress upon yourself that this is exactly what will happen next time the dream occurs. As you fall asleep, remember that your helper will come to you if needed.

4 Enlist your helper, too, to accompany you in any recurring dreams that are pleasant in mood. These often indicate a yearning for further growth. Ask your dream friend to help you to understand the progress that the dream is offering you.

Childhood Dreams

Children dream often and vividly. Indeed, with very small children, it is sometimes hard to tell where dream memories end and waking imagination takes over. But there is no doubt of the fascination that dreaming holds for children, appealing to their love of magic and mystery and promising each night a journey into the unexpected and unexplained.

As children grow, they go through a series of developmental stages, each of which helps a different, specialized kind of learning to take place. It is important to grasp these opportunities because it becomes much harder to learn as we get older. The ability to dream is a case in point. If we encourage our children to remember and to strive to control their dreams early in life, while they are still open-minded, we can save them much effort when they are older.

Teach Your Child to Dream

Children can follow much the same procedures as adults — from keeping a dream diary to using a helper to deal with nightmares. Parents, and other adults close to children, can help them by following a few simple guidelines:

· Invite children to tell you their dreams, and listen carefully. Children learn what is important from the significant adults in their lives.

· Resist the temptation to say to children that their dreams are "silly"; instead, reassure them that their dreams, and their feelings about them, really do matter.

· Confidently suggest to children that they can influence their dreams. This ability depends upon the conviction that it can be done, so try not to sow any doubts in young minds.

· Tell children your own dreams. They love to hear them, and will find the exchange of dreams over the breakfast table both fascinating and constructive.

· Never say that a nightmare was "only a dream" — it is a comforting phrase, but it trivializes the experience. Listen carefully to the child's fears, comfort him or her gently and then explain that

the terrifying creatures we meet in dreams don't really mean to frighten us. Help the child to create a dream helper (see page 123), who will win unpleasant dream creatures over to his or her side.

• Don't try too hard to interpret children's dreams. Welcome them, rather than worry that their dreams reveal parts of themselves that they don't understand. You might, however, explain that a dream event can stand for something else. There is no harm in asking "What do you think this stands for?" or "What do you think this might mean?"

• If the child is really interested in exploring the meaning of dreams, use fairy stories, which have the same archetypal quality as myths and legends, to provide amplification (see page 96). For example, Cinderella is a tale of goodness triumphing over evil and of the transforming power of grace. Jack and the Beanstalk demonstrates that innocence can bring greater rewards than materialism, and demonstrates the value of courage and creative thinking; it also shows our desire to discover the riches of our own minds. Tell your children these stories, discuss their deeper meanings together and encourage the children to watch for their appearance in dreams.

Forbidden Fruit

Case Study 10

 This dream belongs to a young boy, described by his teachers as
rather withdrawn and dreamy.

*" I was walking with some friends past a high wall. I climbed onto it, and saw a
big house with a man standing outside. He said they'd picked all the apples and
they were in the house, and that if I came in I could have some. But I said I was
frightened, and the man called me a coward, and he sounded like my father. I said could
I get my friends to come in with me, but he said no, because they all had
muddy shoes. Then I woke up. "*

The dream reveals several characteristic aspects of childhood. There is the ever-present
sense of being excluded (the high wall), of adventure (climbing the wall) and the love of
forbidden things (the apples in someone else's garden). There is fear, too — of strangers (the
man standing outside); of criticism (being called a coward); of the punitive parent ("he sounded like my father"); and of breaking the rules of the adult world (bringing dirt into
someone else's house). The presence of so many elements in a single dream illustrates the
sometimes confused nature of childhood emotions, and gives adults important clues
about the hectic inner world of the child.

Peer Pressure

Case Study 11

This is a fairly typical anxiety dream, reported by a girl aged 11 — an age when acceptance by one's schoolmates can assume paramount importance.

" Some girls in our class were fighting in the back yard. My mother told me to throw water over them, like we do with cats, so I did. Then they started chasing me. There were some stairs at the back of our house that aren't really there. I ran up, but the stairs became like an escalator going down, and I couldn't climb higher. The girls caught me, and said they would set my hair on fire. They struck some matches, and my head went all hot. I cried out for my mother, and this woke me. "

The dreamer sees adults as authoritarian (her mother decrees that the fighting must stop), and feels that they have little respect for childhood (the mother treats the girls like animals). She has an unthinking obedience to adults (she throws the water over the girls), but she knows that there is no escape from her classmates, and her attempt to flee is pure fantasy (the stairs do not exist, and become an escalator going down). Her fear of being unpopular with the girls in her class, together with an awareness of their vindictiveness, emerges in the nightmare experience of having her hair set alight. The dreamer should be encouraged to discuss her anxieties about being unpopular with her classmates.

Help from the Unconscious

*" Our dreams are most peculiarly
independent of our consciousness and exceedingly valuable
because they cannot cheat. "*
Carl Jung

You are one of your own best teachers. Deep down, no-one knows you better than you know yourself. Much of this self-knowledge is stored in the conscious mind's lifelong companion, the unconscious, a deep reservoir of memories that have long faded from conscious awareness. If you listen to your unconscious, you can tap in to this reserve of knowledge. The practices described in this book, many of them derived from centuries-old traditions, are designed to render this inner teacher readily accessible to you through your dreaming mind.

The final step in the process of teaching yourself to dream is to turn the wisdom of the unconscious outward, toward the issues that affect our well-being and toward our relationships with other people. Our unconscious minds cannot supply the answers to all of the questions that we may have about these subjects: our dreams reflect our intuition and what we have learned in life, but they are not omniscient. We can, however, learn to listen to the insights they provide, and actively

invite them. If the unconscious can find the answers we seek, they may emerge minutes, hours, or even days or weeks later, either in dreams or in waking life. These answers may be hard to interpret, but as Jung implies, the unconscious is an honest broker, unlikely to deceive us in its responses.

Pathways Within

The image of the sea is capable of prompting deep imaginative responses from us all, which might explain why inland dwellers often yearn to visit the coast. Teeming with life and full of surprises, the sea is an apt symbol of the unconscious.

J ust as the creative imagination stems largely from the unconscious, so it can serve as a path back there; following this path, we open up better communication with our inner self and prompt deeper and more intense dream experiences. One way to exercise the imagination is to immerse yourself in the creative insights of others: a visit to an art gallery can provide a wealth of raw material for the creative unconscious. However, more personal results can be obtained by using your own creative powers. It is not necessary to write poems or paint pictures: the creative imagination lies behind all our original thinking.

Creativity can be stimulated in many ways, but the four elements – earth, air, fire and water – provide a good starting point for our imaginings, as they constitute our main archetypal framework for looking at the world. As the tangible building blocks of all animate and inanimate things, the elements occupy an important place in the human psyche.

All four elements are rich in associations, but water particularly so because it is an archetypal symbol of the unconscious itself. In many cultures, sea creatures represent enlightenment: the fish, for example, was the symbol of early Christianity, while the dolphin symbolizes the saviour who carries the soul over the seas of death. The exercise opposite is based on water, but you could equally well design your own exercise around one of the other elements.

Diving with a Dolphin

Dream Exercise 24

This visualization exercise, based on a symbolic submergence into the unconscious,
is designed to open up a broad pathway to bring us into closer contact
with the meaning and mystery within ourselves.

1 Visualize a calm sea on a sunlit day, with a flying fish or a dolphin repeatedly leaping clear of the surface, then diving back underwater.

2 After a moment, plunge into the sea and dive down with the fish or dolphin, accompanying it in your imagination into the depths, past sunken cities and ships, past mermaids and even Neptune himself.

3 Watch the small fish swimming past and feel a oneness with the water, as if you are absorbing some mysterious wisdom through the pores of your being. Listen for the distant music of the sea – the cry of whales, the siren call of mermaids. Know that water, like air, fire and earth, is an elemental part of your body and mind.

4 Allow yourself to drift gently up to the surface and float there, feeling the water lap around you. Breathe gently, feeling the air flow into your lungs. See the shapes of the distant land and feel the heat of the sun. Focus on each of these four elements in turn and think about their different qualities, reminding yourself that the unconscious is as much your home as the conscious mind.

Telling and Listening to Dreams

The old adage that a problem shared is a problem halved applies to dreams just as much as it does to waking life. Talking over your dreams with a friend or partner can help you to remember more details and to arrive at an interpretation. Your listener should be someone you can trust — someone who won't exercise judgment or censure, no matter how bizarre the story.

Encourage friends to recount their dreams in as much detail as they can. Help their recall by asking them to concentrate upon the events just before or after any gap in memory, but resist the temptation to rush in with suggestions of your own.

Start by recounting the dream, trying to recall as much as you can. Next, give your emotional reactions to the dream and its setting. Did you behave as your waking self would have done? If the dream was unfinished, how would you have liked it to end? If it was unsatisfactory in some way, what improvements would you have liked? You can then generate direct associations from the most potent images and events of the dream, and perhaps lead into a discussion of possible overall interpretations.

When listening to others, the important thing is to help the dreamer to remember his or her dreams as fully as possible. Use open questions — such as "How did you feel about this event or character?" or "How would you like the dream to have ended?" — to help your subject to uncover interpretations. Feel free to suggest some ideas of your own, but always express them as questions. For example: "That suggests so-and-so to me; does that make sense?" Never forget that it is the other person's dream, and that in the end, only he or she can interpret it.

Sharing a Daydream

Dream Exercise 25

A valuable way of working with a partner is to share a daydream, by guiding each
other in a joint visualization. Daydreams can be useful structures for important
insights to arise from the unconscious.

1 Tell your partner the destination you wish
to visit – mountains, the shore, an imaginary
city – and be ready to allow him or her to
take you there in your imagination.

2 Your partner should give some details,
but stop frequently to ask you to supply some
of your own. Listen carefully to each other,
building on the details. For example, a trip to
an imaginary city might start like this:

Partner: *You are standing outside the walls of a
great city. The walls are very high, but there is a
large open gate ahead of you, with many people
nearby. What are the people doing?*

Self: *They are wearing medieval costumes, and are
busy buying and selling grain and livestock.*

Partner: *Now enter the city and walk a little way
up one of the streets. You stop to talk to a passer-by.
Who is it? What do you say?*

Self: *She is a frail old woman with a stick, and I
ask her the way to the royal palace. I have an
audience with the King today.*

3 Be prepared for the experience to become
increasingly vivid, and to be surprised by the
things you see. Afterward, many of them can
be interpreted just as with an actual dream.

Relationships

Dream Cue

*Imagine yourself
on a long journey
with your partner.
On the way he or she
is suddenly trans-
formed into a wild
horse. Why should
such a transforma-
tion happen? How do
you persuade the
horse to change back
into your beloved?
Think up your own
answers, and then ask
your dreams for
further variations
on the theme.*

Aspects of relationships often weave a persistent path through our dreams, but because such themes are cloaked in symbols, we may not always recognize the true subject of our dreaming. Even inanimate objects may sometimes represent other people, while other people may represent not themselves but aspects of the dreamer's own psyche. If we can disentangle the messages carried by dreams, then we have a better chance of dealing effectively and honestly with the issues presented by our relationships.

With that aim in mind, talking with one's partner about the possible meanings of a dream can be a helpful way to begin a discussion that might otherwise be difficult or painful to initiate – even if the content of a dream was in fact totally unconnected with the relationship. Start the discussion with the premise that this dream was about your relationship: what does it appear to be saying? Answering the question together can expose areas of disquiet or of potential richness that need to be explored further.

And by discussing the dream in the context of the relationship to which it may have drawn attention, we also offer our dream life a cue for the future, prompting it to provide us with further insights.

As in all areas of dreaming, we cannot be dogmatic about interpretations: the same dream might indicate the destructive nature of a current relationship to one person, but suggest the need to discard old behaviour patterns to another. The exact meaning can only be found through the usual methods of direct association and, if necessary, amplification (see page 96).

If you decide that a dream character actually repre-

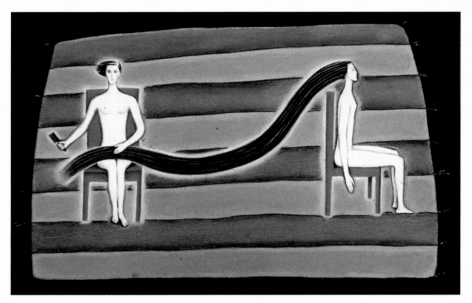

sents the partner or person concerned, think carefully about whether his or her dream behaviour represents hidden attitudes toward you. Because the dream is your creation, it is more likely to be showing you your own unacknowledged insecurities, or drawing your attention to something you may have noticed about the relationship but chosen to ignore. Thus, coldness and withdrawal in a partner's dream persona may highlight your own fears of losing his or her love, and suggest that you look at ways to build up trust or lay anxieties to rest.

When a relationship ends, or when a loved one dies, we often have recurring dreams of losing him or her in crowded places or lonely landscapes. Although these dreams can make us feel sad, they actually help us accept the parting of the ways.

Dreams can also draw attention to people who are potentially important in our lives, by featuring them prominently – and often unexpectedly. Our unconscious mind may have recognized an overlooked potential for shared friendship or interests. In

***Feelings of harmony** with your partner in waking life can be reflected in dreams of simple and tender acts, such as grooming each other.*

much the same way, dreams can draw our attention to someone of whom we should be wary.

In the course of amplification, many relationship dreams provide associations with classical themes, such as the Greek story of Hero and Leander, lovers who lived on opposite sides of the Hellespont strait (better known today as the Dardenelles). Leander swam the Hellespont every night in order to be with Hero, guided by a light that she placed on the shore. One night the light was extinguished by a storm, and Leander drowned; Hero, in deep, suicidal grief, joined him in a watery grave. Such a myth may draw attention to the dangers of passion, or to the suffering experienced when the lamp of love is extinguished.

Unresolved tensions in our relationships can emerge in our dreams. However, you should keep in mind the way in which our unconscious tends to symbolize other difficulties in our lives as relationship problems.

Parents often report anxiety dreams about their children – losing them in crowds, or seeing them injured. These reflect legitimate anxieties, but less clear are dreams in which parents harm their children themselves by an act of deliberate violence. Far from revealing buried hostilities, such dreams often point to the parents' unacknowledged fear that they are somehow stifling or cramping their children. Once the unconscious has brought this concern to the fore, it is for the dreamer to use his or her conscious mind to decide how to proceed.

Finally, dreams can supply the wish-fulfilment that Freud considered was an important aspect of dreaming. Dreams of loving behaviour from those to whom we are attracted or who have grown cold toward us are usually designed to release existing emotional energy, rather than provide guidelines for waking behaviour. Many people find that a careful analysis of their dream relationships is a useful "way in" to understanding the underlying patterns of their emotional lives.

Classifying Dream Relationships

Dream Exercise 26

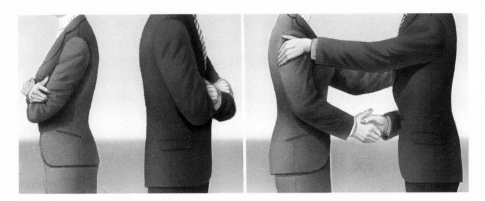

Many dreams about relationships are concerned with specific situations, but dreams can also reveal general information about the way in which our unconscious views our social world. This exercise is designed to help unearth this information.

1 Look back over your dream diary and classify the various characters, both real and imaginary, who have appeared in your dreams. Think about how they behaved and how you felt toward them: for example, were they friendly or hostile, calm or panicky, co-operative or obstinate? List each character under whatever headings seem appropriate.

2 Now note which of the various classifications you have just made predominates. Does your list, for example, suggest an unconscious tendency to see people as generally friendly, or hostile, or critical?

Do your dreams suggest an orientation toward a particular sex or age group?

3 Ask yourself whether these unconscious tendencies are in keeping with your conscious views. A person who sees himself as kind and supportive, for example, might find that his dreams tell a different story.

4 If you feel that your dreams reveal the need to adjust your social behaviour, relive selected dream events in your mind. Picture the characters, who are really projections of your own mind, behaving in more positive ways toward each other.

Dream Sex

A chance encounter with an attractive stranger; a sudden feeling of fondness or passion; making love in public, or outside, or in an unknown place; being seduced by an unattainable object of desire: such erotic fantasies may erupt from the unconscious into vivid dreams. Sometimes we are surprised, even shocked, to find that our dreams express a sexual impulse or attraction that we never acknowledge in our waking life.

Few psychologists would now accept the overwhelming importance attached to sex by Freudian theories. A Jungian view is that many archetypes carry sexual connotations only by virtue of their connection with creativity and fertility. Whichever theory one follows, given the strength of our sexual drives, and the difficulties we often have in coming to terms with them, it is not surprising that sexuality is a prominent theme in dreams.

Sometimes sexual dreams do little more than release sexual tension or energies kept in check during the day, but they can symbolize deeper longings, such as the desire to live in harmony with a loved one. The exercise opposite offers a way to explore these themes, combining the energies of sexuality and visualization to strengthen your emotional bond with a lover.

Dreams of making love can also be an outlet for our wish to express ourselves creatively, to get in closer touch with the feelings and sensitivities represented by the opposite sex (the female aspect of the male, the male aspect of the female), or even to seek union with God, or with the gods.

***Sexual harmony**
is an important
aspect of wholeness.
Perhaps surprisingly,
dreams of farms and
animals often relate
to the archetypal
theme of fertility,
and hence sexuality.*

The Flame of Love

Dream Exercise 27

This intriguing exercise, based on an ancient Tantric technique, is designed to
summon the image of your lover into your dream world.

1 Place a lighted candle on a suitable table
or ledge, and sit about three feet away,
facing it. Close your eyes and breathe
deeply until your mind is calm. Hold the
thought that you are neither waking nor
dreaming, but in a state of consciousness
that embraces both conditions.

2 Open your eyes, look at the candle
flame and gaze at it without blinking.
Visualize the flame taking the shape of the
man or woman you love. It may help to
imagine him or her with arms above the
head, palms together. If the flame flickers,
imagine your lover dancing sinuously, gaz-
ing steadily into your eyes.

3 Keep your mind clear of thoughts,
focusing on the visual experience and staying aware that your mind is embracing
both waking and dreaming. Know that,
because of this, the loved one will appear
in your dreams.

4 Continue the exercise for at least five
minutes, and try to repeat it every day,
lengthening it if possible to 15 minutes or
more. Keep the eyes as still and the mind as
empty as possible.

5 When you are practised at this technique, visualize the flame disappearing,
leaving the loved one in front of you.

Toward Well-being

On average, we remember two unpleasant dreams for every pleasant dream that we recall. Disturbing dreams are not in themselves a sign of psychological turmoil. The unconscious has simply used an alarming dream to draw attention to unsatisfactory aspects of our inner lives: it knows that the situation is not ideal, and that something should be done about it.

One of the main aspects of mental well-being is the ability to face change and the insecurities and uncertainties that change brings. Dreams often become particularly vivid and disturbing in times of major upheaval, such as adolescence, changing jobs, marriage, parenthood, divorce, bereavement and retirement. Such dreams represent part of the process of unconscious adjustment, but they can also give valuable guidance on the way ahead.

Sad dreams may reflect our inner feelings of loss as our lives move on, forcing us to leave behind things we have cherished in the past.

Encourage these dreams to be more positive by reflecting or meditating daily upon symbols of transformation such as the changing seasons, rebirth, metamorphosis and regeneration. Immerse yourself in myths involving these themes, such as the

tales of Isis and Osiris, Demeter and Persephone, Cupid and Psyche, even Sleeping Beauty. Impress upon your unconscious that you accept the dynamism and renewal that change can bring, and your dreams will tend to present these issues in a more positive light.

Psychological well-being underpins our ability to work, relax and relate to others. Dreams cannot provide the answers to all our psychological problems: sometimes all they can do is reveal the presence of buried conflicts and confusions which have to be resolved at the conscious level, and probably with the help of others.

Dreams can often help to monitor and even accelerate the healing process during illness, and especially during recuperation, but they are obviously no substitute for proper medical care. If you are recovering from illness or from surgery, spend time before sleep focusing your mind and instruct your unconscious to give your physical body all the energy and freedom enjoyed by your dreaming body. The very act of willing the dream body to health has benefits in waking life. Exercise 28, on the next page, suggests a simple way to help us track our progress toward general well-being and identify where improvements can be made.

Dreams can also help us to come to terms with long-term difficulties, such as frequent migraines or deterioration of hearing or eyesight. In these cases, dreams can help us to replace a negative, defeatist attitude with a positive, optimistic one, based on a recognition of our limitations and a reminder of the potential that remains uncompromised. Ask your dreams to help you to develop (or maintain) this attitude, and to achieve the frame of mind best suited to healing – for example, by banishing the excessive self-criticism that can hinder progress toward full health.

Regardless of whether or not you remember a healing dream, remember to thank your unconscious the following morning for its help. Many of our dreams vanish without trace, and the healing process may be under way without your knowledge. Don't forget that the unconscious responds to praise and encouragement, and appreciates being reassured that you continue to have confidence in it.

Dream cue

To help develop the restorative frame of mind that speeds recuperation, try to visualize before sleep a special healing place — maybe a large, sunny, calm room, or a mountain resort surrounded by vistas of pure white snow. Vow to visit the place in your dreams, and know that you will benefit from its curative powers.

Summoning a Healing Metaphor

Dream Exercise 28

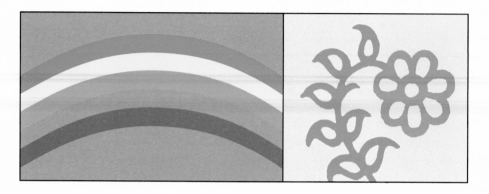

The identification of a healing metaphor – a personal symbol of the healing process itself – can be a valuable catalyst to the process of recuperation. This symbol can present itself to your dreaming mind in a wide range of forms.

1 Before sleep, scan your recent dreams for a symbol of an unresolved health problem. In order to elucidate such symbols, you may need to apply the procedures of direct association and amplification (see pages 78 and 96).

2 Focus on the health problem, and ask your dreaming mind to provide you with a healing metaphor which will not only give your conscious mind more confidence in the healing process, but will also help to mobilize your inner power to heal yourself. Remember that dreams are one way to reprogram the unconscious.

3 Watch your subsequent dreams for the appearance of this healing metaphor. You may, for example, dream of putting on new clothes, of flowers, of taking a bath, or of a beautiful rainbow. Focus upon the metaphor as often as possible during waking hours, and visualize it replacing your earlier anxiety dreams.

4 Hold the image in your mind before going to sleep. Even if it does not re-appear in the same form in your dreams, it can still influence the direction of the dreaming mind – and at the same time provide a mental model for the healing process.

Healing the Dream Body

Dream Exercise 29

One of the obstacles to healing is that we incorporate our health problem into our self-image. In our minds we *become* a person with a bad back, or with migraine or skin problems, or whatever. Block this process by thinking of yourself as fit and well again.

1 When you are ill, be it with a short-term illness such as influenza or a longer-term problem, think of an activity such as running along the seashore or through the woods, and imagine doing it without difficulty. Visualize yourself looking in the mirror and seeing yourself restored to health.

2 Remind yourself that in the dream world, illness can be banished at will. If your dream body also suffers your physical problem, believe that it will soon be fully recovered. Tell your dreaming mind that you want to feel as well as possible, within the limits imposed by your illness.

3 Notice any improvements in your dream body that take place as a consequence, and tell yourself that you can achieve similar results with your physical body.

4 Remember that the ancient Greeks saw healing as one of the main functions of dreaming. Feel confident that your dreams can also provide guidance on the healing process. Just as the Greeks believed that priests could use dream divination to bring such guidance, persuade yourself that there is a benevolent influence associated with your dreams which has the wisdom and power to assist the healing process.

The Fulfilled Dreamer

There is no end to the study of dreaming. Whether we agree with the Tibetan Buddhist belief that dreams are a dress rehearsal for the next world, or are happy to adopt the view expressed in this book that they are the royal road to the unconscious, they undoubtedly represent an inner dimension of mystery, enchantment and wisdom. They are our most undervalued route to personal fulfilment.

Our dreams represent our attempt to reconcile our conscious and unconscious minds. Nature intends us to live in harmony with ourselves, and wants peace and understanding to reign between the different levels of ourselves. Thus, dreams show our conscious mind ways to free the unconscious from the bonds of everyday life, suggesting ways to help us hear messages from the unconscious and to understand their true meaning.

Dreams are a creative process that can change the way in which we view ourselves, our relationships and the material world, answering the question "Who am I?" which is at the heart of our search for meaning. Their very "otherness" is a constant challenge to conventional ways of thinking and being, offering a chance to see beyond the prosaic confines of everyday life, while at the same time giving us valuable insights into our inner world.

Progress in dreaming and progress in life often go hand in hand: each reflects and illuminates the other. As we teach ourselves to dream, we will notice that our dreams become increasingly coherent, adding meaning to each other to make an ever more complete picture. Our dreams will respond more readily to the requests made of them in waking life. Gone will be much of the fragmentation

and the absurdities that characterize untutored dreaming. Instead, dreams will take on an increasingly numinous and memorable quality, as if giving you insights into a superior way of being, and lucid dreams will tend to become more frequent and coherent. Also, you will find it progressively easier to interpret your dreams, both because you have learned the language of dreaming, and because your dreaming mind will recognize that you are looking to it for guidance.

If the world were no more than what our senses can discover, our dreams would never venture beyond the mundane and the predictable. They would tie us to our worldly concerns, instead of freeing us to explore the rich, mysterious realm of the unconscious. In order to enter the inner kingdom of the mind, we need only to follow the path of dreams, keeping our eyes and minds open, ready and willing to do our utmost to understand the images and symbols revealed on the way.

*A **garden** of inner peace rests within each of us. Once we have found the key to it in our dreams, we should visit it regularly, guarding it carefully against intrusions by unwelcome or stressful thoughts.*

An A–Z of Dream Symbols

Dreaming is a genuinely personal experience. As we delve into our individual dream worlds, we discover a system of symbols that is unique to ourselves. This brief survey of some common dream symbols offers some broad interpretations intended to serve as starting points for your own analysis.

Air This element is associated with clarity of thought and wisdom lightly worn. We may find ourselves bounding in great leaps across the countryside, floating down to earth, or travelling in a balloon or on a cloud. Air symbolizes otherworldly concerns, but may also be warning of the danger of losing contact with reality.

Armour To dream of wearing heavy clothing or armour may indicate that the dreamer is being over-defensive in his or her life. With more self-confidence and openness, we might not have to take such extreme measures to protect ourselves from the outside world.

Bird The dove stands for peace and reconciliation. Territorial birds (such as blackbirds) can represent jealousy, while thieving birds (such as magpies) may suggest a threat from an outsider, or aspects of the self stolen by a friend or partner. A newly hatched bird (or egg) can indicate new possibilities in life – or the need for nurturing.

Blood This can connote the life-force within us; spilled blood represents its sacrifice and loss.

Book This variously represents wisdom, the intellect, or the historical record of the dreamer's life. Inability to read a book could mean that the dreamer needs to develop a greater level of concentration and awareness in waking life.

Bureaucracy Dealing with bureaucracy in dreams often relates to lack of emotion, either in the dreamer or in those whom he or she meets. The dream may be urging a more personal, committed approach to relationships. Otherwise, it may be emphasizing the dreamer's helplessness at understanding complex issues, or signifying that more attention to detail is necessary.

Castle To dream of being inside a castle suggests security, but can also remind us that the very strength of our psychological defences may be isolating us from others.

Cat This may stand for the imaginative power of the dreamer's unconscious, or his or her intuitive feminine side. If the cat is known to the dreamer, the significance of the dream will be more personal.

Chase Dreams of being chased by an unseen but terrifying presence usually indicate that aspects of the self are clamouring for integration into consciousness. The dreamer should try to turn and face the pursuer, gaining clues as to what this symbol represents.

Circle This is the classic symbol of infinity, the void, the ineffable and the unknowable. It can also signify the female principle, entry into the mysteries, or a sense of completion.

City A ruined city may be drawing the dreamer's attention to a neglect of relationships, aims or ideals in life. Ruins generally suggest neglect and decay rather than deliberate destruction.

Classroom This can represent learning, but also competition, public esteem or the need to re-think aspects of one's personal or professional concerns. It may simply reflect nostalgia for an earlier stage of life, or the dreamer's need to re-kindle the joy, passion or ambition he or she felt then.

Cloak A particularly ambivalent dream symbol, the cloak can stand for concealment and secrecy, for mystery and the occult, or for protective warmth and love. Freudian psychology associates the cloak with enveloping female sexuality.

Clock Timepieces stand for the heart, and the emotional side of life. A stopped clock indicates a cooling or stilling of the emotions, while a clock racing out of control suggests emotions that may be overwhelming the conscious mind.

Clown The clown is an aspect of the archetypal Trickster (see page 92), making a fool of himself or herself to mock the pretentiousness and absurd posturing of others.

Colours See page 46.

Crack This suggests flaws in the dreamer's character, or defects in certain of his or her arguments, ideas or relationships. A cracked or broken vase or cup may symbolize lost love.

Cup On the one hand, the cup is a classic Freudian symbol of female sexuality. On the other hand, through its associations with the Arthurian legend of the Holy Grail, the cup may also stand for the abstract qualities of love and truth.

Dancing In Level 1 and 2 dreams, dancing can represent courtship, or stand as a metaphor for sexual intercourse. In Level 3 dreams it often symbolizes the rhythms of life, the powers of creation and destruction or the unlimited creative power of the imagination.

Dog This can be a symbol of loyalty and faithfulness (representing a need for protection or friendship), or of scarcely-tamed wildness. If the dreamer encounters a dog that belongs to someone he or she knows, the feelings that person inspires could be transferred to the dog.

Doll This may represent the Anima or Animus (see page 91), the qualities of the opposite sex within us. Jung also found that dolls sometimes indicate lack of communication between the conscious and unconscious levels of the mind.

Domination Bondage can, of course, have overtly erotic overtones in a dream, reflecting sexual urges in the dreamer that are perhaps unacknowledged by the waking mind. However, in a non-sexual context it can also suggest repressed spiritual aspirations.

Drowning Dreams of drowning, or struggling in deep water, may represent the dreamer's fear of being engulfed by forces hidden in the deepest reaches of the unconscious mind. Such dreams often indicate that control over the unconscious needs to be relaxed slowly.

Earth Dreams of sitting or lying on the ground suggest the importance of realism, a need to end flights of fancy. The earth can also symbolize fertility, and, like water, can represent the feminine. Barren earth can hint that new ideas are imminent: the old ground must be ploughed up and sown with the seeds of new life.

Egg See Bird.

Eyes Symbolic windows into the soul, eyes can provide clues to the spiritual condition of the dreamer, or of the people encountered in dreams. Bright eyes suggest a healthy inner life.

Falling Anxiety dreams often place us in situations in which we are powerless to act. Among the most common is the dream of falling from a great height, an image that emphasizes that the dreamer has climbed very high in personal or professional life and may now be afraid of failure.

Fire A powerful and ambivalent dream symbol. Fire destroys, but it also cleanses and purifies. In dreams it represents the overt, the positive and the conscious, and can signal new beginnings, or represent disruptive emotions – such as passion or envy. Out of control, however, fire may suggest the need to curb unbridled emotions or ambition.

Food For Freud, food represented the two vital life-instincts – self-preservation, (greed) and species preservation (sex). He saw the mouth as the primary erogenous zone, and fasting and gorging as symbols of sexual desire (respectively denied or indulged). Fruit can represent creativity (bearing fruit), sensuality, and rewards; milk has connotations of kindness and nourishment; and honey (the food of the gods, according to many traditions) is a symbol of wealth and contentment.

Fractured limb This represents a threat to the foundations of life, or suggest anxieties about the safety of intimates.

Funeral Burial may denote an end, or the need for an end, to a particular phase of the dreamer's life, or represent the repression of desires and traumas. Where the funeral is not associated with someone known to us, it can be a reminder of the passing of time, or of the importance of not establishing too many emotional attachments.

Ghost The shadowy image of a ghost may suggest fear of death, or knowledge within the dreamer that now requires fleshing out by the conscious mind. Dreams of ghostly figures hovering over the dreamer's sleeping body are sometimes interpreted as out-of-body experiences, in which the dreamer's "soul" sheds its physical form.

Giant For children, giants often represent dominant adults in their lives who have what may seem infinite and arbitrary power. By confronting these monsters in dreams, children come to terms with them in their emotional lives. For adults, giants may represent childhood memories. Although dream giants are awe-inspiring, some may symbolize care and protection.

Gift A gift that appears inappropriate to the dreamer may indicate the unwelcome attentions of another person, or qualities or virtues in the dreamer of which he or she feels unworthy; if the dreamer is the giver rather than the recipient, the dream may be a reminder to present one's weaknesses – or true nature – more accurately to others.

Hair In dreams, hair often symbolizes vanity; the ritual act of shaving the head indicates a renunciation of worldly ways. Early dream interpreters suggested that to dream of going bald predicts an imminent loss of the heart. A strong beard can stand for vitality, a white one can represent age, experience or wisdom.

Heart The heart carries archetypal significance as the centre of emotional life, and in particular as the symbol of love.

Horse This generally symbolizes humankind's harnessing of the wild forces of nature. A winged or flying horse can represent the unleashing of energy for psychological or spiritual growth. In Freudian interpretation, a wild horse represents the dreaded, terrifying aspect of the *alter ego*.

Hotel Icons of impermanence, hotels may symbolize a time of transition in a relationship, a shift of personal identity or even the loss of it.

House This often represents the dreamer, or those things that give life stability and orientation. Empty or dark windows suggest the extinction not only of the loved one but also of vital aspects of the dreamer's conscious life. An unfinished house, or one in poor repair, may be pointing out to the dreamer that work is required on some aspects of mind or body.

Interview Oral examinations can be even more anxiety-provoking than written ones. The interviewers facing the dreamer may represent aspects of the self, suggesting self-rejection, self-dissatisfaction or perhaps simply that the dreamer needs to undertake a searching review of his or her priorities. To be tongue-tied in the face of the panel may suggest that the dreamer has no convincing answer to the voice of conscience.

Isolated place Seeking an island or a deserted place reflects a craving for solitude, or a conviction that most problems in life come from the activities of other people. Choosing to stay on an island – opting for exile – can also suggest a wish to cling to consciousness instead of venturing out onto the sea of the unconscious.

Jewels These suggest a valued aspect of the dreamer or of other people. Gold and diamonds typically represent the incorruptible true self, rubies denote passion, sapphires truth, and emeralds fertility. Jewels may also represent buried treasure, the archetype of divine wisdom hidden in the depths of the collective unconscious.

Journey Freud considered that the smooth motion of a car was a symbol of progress in psychoanalysis. Sea travel may represent a journey into the deep waters of the unconscious. Either way, travel is a common symbol of personal growth and exploration.

Knife The knife or dagger is by far the most common male sexual symbol, its ability to penetrate paralleled by the penis in sexual intercourse. The knife can stand for masculinity in its associations with violence and aggression. It may also represent the "sword of truth" that cuts through falsity and ignorance, or the will to cut away false desires.

Liberation Dreams of freeing someone may indicate the dreamer's altruistic urge to serve that person by releasing him or her from psychological bondage. Freeing animals from captivity, by contrast, more often relates to releasing the dreamer's own emotions or primal energies.

Library A library typically represents the world of ideas, and the ready availability of knowledge. To be distracted by other readers, or to fail to find a book, may indicate the need for more concentration or discrimination.

Light For Jung, light in dreams "always refers to consciousness". Such dreams suggest profound insights illuminating the conscious mind. Through amplification of these dreams, the dreamer may find religious or mythical associations – for example, with Christ as the light of the world, or the divine boundless light of Eastern belief, or the sun god Apollo.

Lion Almost invariably appearing in dreams as a regal symbol of power and pride, the lion often represents the archetypal, powerful and admired aspect of the father.

Mask Generally masks represent the way that we present ourselves to the outside world and even to ourselves. If the dreamer is unable to remove a mask, or is forced by others to wear one, this suggests that the real self is becoming increasingly obscured.

Maze This usually relates to the dreamer's progress into the unconscious. Getting lost in a maze may represent the complex defences put up by the conscious ego to prevent unconscious wishes and desires from emerging into the light.

Mermaid Combining the symbolism of fish and femininity, the mermaid is a powerful image of the mysterious otherness that haunts and fascinates the male psyche. In dreams, a mermaid typically embodies the Anima (see page 91) – a bringer of secret wisdom and a seductive temptress, luring the energies of the conscious mind into the uncharted depths of the unconscious.

Mirror Seeing your own face in the mirror may be a sign of narcissism or egotism, while a strange face in the mirror often indicates identity crisis. If the face is startling or frightening, it may stand for the Shadow (see page 93).

Misbehaviour Dreams in which the dreamer deliberately breaks rules often hark back to early childhood. The dreamer's natural urge toward self-assertion and testing the limits imposed by others may have been restricted by parents or other

adults, and his or her repressed rebellious nature may still lie in the unconscious, asserting itself by dream transgressions.

Money Hoarding money in dreams indicates either prudence or selfishness. Freud considered that it was a sign of anal fixation, but it may also be an indication of insecurity. Being short of money, or unable to find any, can symbolize shortage of energy or time. Sharing wealth shows altruism and magnanimity.

Monkey This animal often represents the dreamer's playful, mischievous side, and may symbolize an immature yet instinctively wise aspect of consciousness that requires some means of expression. The monkey can also symbolize the untamed, chattering mind that needs to be stilled by meditation.

Moon A symbol of mystery and femininity, the moon is the queen of the night. It is also associated with water (tides are governed by the moon), and with imagination. Dreams of a full moon may indicate serenity and stillness, signifying the dreamer's potential for contemplation. A new moon is an obvious symbol of fresh beginnings.

Mountain Climbing mountains may suggest sexual activity or aspirations, the male aspects of the self, or else spiritual progress.

Mouth For Freud, dreams about mouths represented an early stage of psychosexual development, marked by immature characteristics such as gullibility or verbal aggression.

Music Beautiful music in dreams can symbolize the infinite potential of creative life, the heavenly "music of the spheres" of the Greeks and Romans. By contrast, the chaos and confusion of discordant music suggests creative potential that has been neglected or become distorted.

Nudity   To dream of being naked in a public place among people who are unconcerned indicates that we should discard fears of being rejected. To be disgusted at another's nudity suggests anxiety or aversion at discovering their real nature; accepting the nudity of others indicates the dreamer's ability to perceive their true qualities. In Level 3 dreams nudity can represent the dreamer's spirituality or true self.

Painting   While successful painting can represent the dreamer's creative potential, unsuccessful attempts indicate creativity seeking expression, or inner turmoil or uncertainty. Vivid colours may stand for unconscious energy, while drab ones can indicate a veil between the dreamer and his or her insight (for more on colours, see pages 46–47).

Police   Law officers can be reassuring in dreams, but equally may represent the dreamer's inhibitions, and the censorship of natural impulses by the conscious mind. Being chased by the police can indicate a need to face the accusations of a guilty conscience, or to learn from past mistakes.

Privacy   If the dreamer is anxious that a place lacks privacy, this may indicate the fear of public exposure, or the need for better self-expression.

Prize   Trophies carry a value far beyond their material worth – just as a cup's value is not intrinsic, but depends upon what it can hold. In dreams, even if the nature of the prize remains obscure, the sense of triumph is normally unmistakable.

Puppet   Glove puppets or marionettes suggest manipulation and a lack of free choice. The dreamer may discover that they stand as a symbol of the wish for power over others, or a lack of control in his or her own life – a typically punning dream reference to the cliché that somebody else is pulling the strings.

Rainbow   Universally auspicious symbols, rainbows stand for redemption, good news, promise and forgiveness. In Level 3 dreams they can be associated with the magical quest for the treasure of self-knowledge, or for the bridge between heaven and earth that awaits the enlightened mind.

Rose   As well as being the traditional symbol of love, the red rose in Freud's view often indicates the female genitalia, or alternatively the blood of menstruation.

Sea   Jung believed that turning to face the sea indicates that the dreamer is prepared to confront the unconscious, while creatures emerging from the deep represent powerful archetypal forces. For Freud, the sea and the incoming tide were primal symbols of sexual union.

Shell   This is a profoundly spiritual symbol that often represents the unconscious, and through its links with the sea, the imagination. Shells may also stand for shyness or protective barriers (withdrawing into your shell) or for a feeling of hollowness (an empty shell).

Shoes   Some dreamers who report seeing shoes or boots in their dreams associate them with sexuality: like cups, hats and gloves, they can be entered by other parts of the body. Women's shoes can sometimes stand for dominant female sexuality, which may come from the infant's experience of crawling close to his or her mother's feet.

Slope The relatively common dream in which we attempt to climb a descending escalator, a slippery slope or a greasy ladder suggests failure to make progress in a desired area, and may serve as a reminder either to abandon the attempt or to seek a more appropriate way up. See also Mountain.

Snow Melting snow suggests fears and obstacles dissolving, but snow can also symbolize transformation and purification. A dream of icy, freezing conditions can indicate delay, or an obstacle in the way of the mind's creative flow. It may also suggest that the dreamer has paid insufficient attention to his or her own feelings.

Spider In dreams the devouring mother, who consumes her children through possessiveness or her power to arouse guilt, is often symbolized by the spider, who traps and lives off her innocent victims.

Star As well as representing fate and the celestial powers, the stars can stand for the dreamer's higher states of consciousness. A single star shining more brightly than the rest can signify success in competition, but may also be the one that is closest to destruction.

Station or airport These and other points of departure can indicate a wide choice of possibilities, the meeting of ideas, or apprehensions or excitement about the future.

Sun Archetypal symbol of the masculine, the sun stands for the conscious mind, the intellect, and the father. A hot sun can indicate the intellect's power to make a desert out of the dreamer's emotional life. Conversely, the sun hidden by clouds can suggest that the dreamer's emotions overrule rational thought processes.

Teeth Dental problems, such as teeth falling out, being broken, and so on, are the focus of many anxiety dreams, reflecting insecurities in the personal, domestic or professional sphere.

Temple A temple, church or other place of worship can represent peace, higher wisdom or the spiritual side of the dreamer. To feel that one is a stranger inside a church may remind the dreamer to attend to the spiritual dimension.

Toilet The need to excrete in dreams usually represents the dreamer's public anxiety, or his or her urgent wish to express or unburden the self. Searching for a toilet may indicate conflict between the need to express oneself and fear of what might emerge if one does. Finding a toilet engaged indicates jealousy of another's position or creativity; while causing a toilet to overflow indicates fear about losing control, or failure to discipline creativity.

Train Trains follow a fixed route, suggesting that the dreamer is receiving help on his or her journey. Being on the wrong train or passing one's destination can denote missed opportunities.

Transformation A change from winter to summer may indicate deep transformations within the dreamer. Movement in the opposite direction may suggest the need for a fallow period or for more communication with the unconscious. Transition from day to night may carry a similar message. Bridges are a classic symbol of change, spanning the boundary between past and future.

Underclothes These may represent unconscious attitudes and prejudices, their colour and condition giving clues to the specific details. Shame at being seen in underclothes can indicate a reluctance to have these attitudes made public.

Vacation To dream of making preparations for a vacation generally suggests a need to escape from everyday problems, or to seek new excitements and experiences. A wish to travel light can indicate recognition of the unnecessary "baggage" that we usually carry with us in life. Anxiety about how much to take away may represent a fear of, or preoccupation with, death.

Violence toward others This often represents a struggle for self-assertion, or a fight against unwanted aspects of the dreamer's inner or outer life. Violence against a child can represent failure to accept the child in oneself, while violence toward an older man or woman may indicate a refusal to listen to the wisdom of others.

Violence toward the self Dreams in which the dreamer finds himself or herself violently attacked often represent a sense of guilt, and a desire for self-punishment. They can also indicate that the dreamer is too vulnerable or apprehensive in the face of the outside world, as if outer forces are battering him or her into quiet submission.

Wall High enclosures or impenetrable fences around a city, or around an individual house, suggest exclusiveness, a wish to keep others out and a desire to protect one's treasured possessions. The dream may be suggesting that a wall is necessary if social values are to be maintained, or it may be inviting the dreamer to recognize that a wall exists and to question its usefulness.

War Jung interpreted dreams of wars as signs of major conflict between aspects of the conscious and unconscious minds. Such dreams are likely to reflect a struggle between deep instinctive forces and rules of conscious conduct; they may indicate a need for reconciliation rather than victory.

Watch See Clock.

Water The symbol par excellence of the unconscious, water in all its forms suggests the depths of the imagination. To dream of swimming suggests that the dreamer should venture into this realm, but dreams of sinking may be a warning that more preparation is required. A flowing tap (faucet), or similar, is often a symbol of ejaculation, and may denote new creativity.

Wedding Marriage often suggests the union of opposite yet complementary parts of the self, and the promise of future fertility. It may be of arche-typal significance, symbolizing the union within the dreamer of the fundamental creative forces of life – male and female, rationality and imagina-tion, conscious and unconscious, matter and spirit.

Whip Although a whip in dreams can be a negatively charged symbol of sexual submission, more generally it can represent the dreamer's awareness of power, domination and obedience in the pattern of his or her relationships.

Wild beast Freud considered that ferocious, untamed animals represent passionate impulses of which the dreamer is ashamed; the more numerous and diverse the animals, the more varied and threatening these impulses may be.

Window Both doors and windows were seen by Freud as feminine sexual symbols; but Jung associated them with the ability to understand the outside world. Looking in through windows (voyeurism for Freud) can suggest the dreamer substitutes curiosity for self-examination.

Winning a race This indicates a recognition of potential within ourselves. To come second or third may suggest aspirations beyond one's means.

Index

Photo Credits